Encouraging Economic Diversification in Libya Through Public-Private Dialogues

LESSONS LEARNED FROM 2020-2023

OECD
BETTER POLICIES FOR BETTER LIVES

Please cite this publication as:
OECD (2025), *Encouraging Economic Diversification in Libya Through Public-Private Dialogues: Lessons Learned from 2020-2023*, OECD Publishing, Paris, https://doi.org/10.1787/ed7bb2e0-en.

ISBN 978-92-64-72960-5 (print)
ISBN 978-92-64-50084-6 (PDF)
ISBN 978-92-64-41377-1 (HTML)

Revised version, October 2026
Details of revisions available at: https://www.oecd.org/en/publications/support/corrigenda.html

Photo credits: Cover © Claudiovidri/Shutterstock.com.

Corrigenda to OECD publications may be found at: https://www.oecd.org/en/publications/support/corrigenda.html.

Foreword

This report is part of a broader EU-OECD initiative aimed at strengthening economic resilience and inclusive governance in Libya; a key component of the longstanding MENA-OECD Initiative on Governance and Competitiveness for Development. Since 2013, the OECD has been working with Libyan institutions and partners to support post-conflict recovery, economic diversification, and institutional capacity development. Through earlier engagements under the G7 Deauville Partnership and more recent cooperation with the European Union, OECD's work has contributed to enhancing Libya's business climate, supporting small and medium-sized enterprises (SMEs), and strengthening human and institutional capacities.

In 2019, the OECD launched the project "Promoting Public-Private Dialogue (PPD) in Libya" to foster inclusive economic governance by encouraging structured dialogue between the public and private sectors. Over the course of its implementation (2020–2023), the project mobilised more than 200 Libyan stakeholders across key economic sectors such as agribusiness, banking and finance, ICT, infrastructure, and transport and logistics. Through more than 45 consultation sessions held in Tripoli, Benghazi, Misrata, and Sabha, this inclusive approach ensured broad geographic representation and enabled Libyan actors from diverse regions to articulate challenges, co-create policy solutions, and contribute to national economic development goals.

The project draws on the OECD's methodology on Public-Private Dialogue, which promotes inclusive and structured engagement between governments and economic actors. In fragile and post-conflict settings like Libya, inclusive dialogue platforms are critical tools to rebuild trust, foster policy coherence, and bridge institutional divides. The initiative has also prioritised capacity building and peer learning, connecting Libyan stakeholders with regional counterparts and exposing them to international good practices in regulatory reform, digital transformation, and private sector development.

We are especially grateful for the generous support of the European Union and the close collaboration of Libyan partners from public institutions, business associations, and civil society. We also extend our appreciation to Tatweer Research, the OECD's local implementing partner, whose engagement and network-building efforts have been instrumental in ensuring the project's regional reach and impact.

This report synthesises the main outcomes of the PPD project, including sector-specific analyses, key challenges identified by stakeholders, and actionable policy recommendations aimed at supporting Libya's path toward economic resilience and inclusive growth. It also outlines opportunities for sustaining dialogue mechanisms and deepening reform momentum in the years to come.

The OECD remains committed to accompanying Libya on its path toward recovery and development, through ongoing technical assistance, policy dialogue, and regional cooperation. We look forward to deepening our collaboration with Libyan and international partners to build on the achievements of this initiative and support the emergence of a dynamic, inclusive, and sustainable Libyan economy.

Acknowledgements

This report was produced under the framework of the EU-OECD project on *Promoting Public-Private Dialogue in Libya*, implemented under the overall guidance and leadership of Carlos Conde, Head of the Middle East and Africa Division at the OECD.

This project was funded by the European Union. The contents of this report are the sole responsibility of the OECD and do not necessarily reflect the views of the European Union. The OECD gratefully acknowledges the financial support of the European Union Delegation to Libya.

This project was carried out with the contribution of the Directorate General for Political Affairs and International Security of the Italian Ministry of Foreign Affairs and International Cooperation, pursuant to Directorial Decree No. 343 of 26/07/2023. The opinions expressed in this publication are the sole responsibility of the OECD do not necessarily reflect the positions of the Italian Ministry of Foreign Affairs and International Cooperation. The OECD gratefully acknowledges the financial support of the Italian Ministry of Foreign Affairs and International Cooperation.

The OECD is grateful to its Libyan counterparts for their close collaboration and valuable contributions. In particular, we would like to thank the Ministry of Economy and Trade, notably Mr Mussa Ezubik and Mr Hassan Al-Kamel, for their active engagement and support.

The OECD also extends its appreciation to the project's consultant and experts, including Tatweer Research, Esam Garba and Saleh Meylod, whose expertise and insights were instrumental in the development of this report.

This document was drafted by the project team within the Middle East and Africa Division, Global Relations and Cooperation Directorate, comprising Mohammed Baraka, Roger Fores Carrion, Rania Ampntel Chafiz, Tarek Jalleb and Sophie Elliott. The document also benefited from the guidance and review of Mariarosa Lunati, Max Bulakovskiy and Heekyung Jun.

The OECD acknowledges with gratitude the contributions of all partners and experts who supported this work and helped advance the dialogue on economic resilience and private sector development in Libya.

Table of contents

FIGURES

TABLES

BOXES

Executive Summary

Libya's economy continues to face long-standing challenges, with limited diversification and a business environment still largely shaped by the state. In an effort to open space for reform, the EU-OECD Project on Promoting Public-Private Dialogue (PPD) brought together people from across the public and private sectors in four cities—Tripoli, Benghazi, Misrata, and Sebha. Through a series of conversations and workshops, the project helped identify practical solutions in five key sectors, while building trust between institutions and businesses. These efforts came together in a final national dialogue, where participants outlined shared priorities for moving the economy forward.

This report presents key findings and policy recommendations across five priority sectors of the Libyan economy: Banking and Financial Services, Agribusiness, Information and Communication Technology (ICT), Infrastructure and Construction, and Transport and Logistics. These sectors were selected for their potential to drive economic diversification, support job creation, and strengthen Libya's resilience in a fragile and rapidly evolving environment. Each chapter draws on targeted public-private dialogue sessions and OECD good practices to assess challenges, identify reform priorities, and propose actionable solutions.

Banking and Financial Services

The Libyan banking sector remains underdeveloped and heavily reliant on public banks with limited private sector participation. Challenges include a weak regulatory framework, limited access to credit—especially for SMEs—and the absence of a national financial inclusion strategy. Stakeholders highlighted the urgent need to modernise the banking infrastructure, introduce credit guarantee mechanisms, strengthen supervisory capacity, and promote digital and mobile banking solutions. Enhancing financial literacy and developing tailored financial products for entrepreneurs and start-ups were also prioritised.

Agribusiness

Despite Libya's vast arable land and a strong domestic demand for food products, the agribusiness sector suffers from inadequate irrigation infrastructure, fragmented value chains, outdated regulatory frameworks, and limited private investment. Public-private dialogue participants emphasised the need to improve land tenure systems, enhance access to agricultural finance, develop agro-processing capabilities, and invest in cold chain logistics. Enabling conditions for contract farming, market access, and rural entrepreneurship—especially for youth and women—were seen as essential to revitalising the sector.

Information and Communication Technology (ICT)

Libya's ICT sector holds significant potential for growth and job creation, but is constrained by weak digital infrastructure, monopolistic market structures, and outdated legislation. Participants across regions called for liberalising the sector, improving digital connectivity—especially in underserved areas—and introducing a robust legal framework for data protection, cybersecurity, and e-governance. Strategic investments in digital skills development and support for the start-up ecosystem were identified as critical enablers for a competitive digital economy.

Infrastructure and Construction

Infrastructure gaps in transportation, energy, and utilities are among the main barriers to private sector development in Libya. Years of underinvestment, conflict-related damage, and inconsistent urban planning have disrupted service delivery and increased business costs. Dialogue sessions underlined the need for a national infrastructure strategy, greater transparency in project selection, and mechanisms to crowd in private investment, including through public-private partnerships (PPPs). Streamlining procurement processes and strengthening municipal capacity were highlighted as urgent reform areas.

Transport and Logistics

The transport sector, once a strategic connector between Africa and Europe, has suffered from years of neglect and insecurity. Fragmented governance, outdated facilities, and the lack of multimodal integration have constrained trade and mobility. Stakeholders stressed the importance of rehabilitating key transport corridors, modernising customs and border procedures, and developing regulatory frameworks for logistics services. Investment in ports, intermodal hubs, and digital transport solutions were viewed as critical to restoring Libya's position as a regional trade gateway.

1 The Economic context in Libya

Libya's protracted conflict has brought the economy to a critical juncture. Historical legacies and ongoing disruptions hinder development and reinforce deep structural vulnerabilities[1]. The conflict has significantly impacted the private sector, leaving enduring challenges that permeate various facets of the business landscape. However, as seen in many post-conflict situations, the private sector, while suffering in its potential for sustainability and growth, also plays a key role in resilience ensuring the provision of goods and services and finding alternative ways to maintain the economic structure of the country. This note describes the conditions of five strategic sectors and provides some policy orientations to improve the business climate and, in turn, enhance the economic performance of the country.

Before the conflict erupted, Libya's economic structure was predominantly state-driven, heavily reliant on oil revenues, with over 95% of export revenues deriving from the hydrocarbons sector (World Bank, 2021[1]). The dominance of state-owned enterprises, lack of competition, policy unpredictability, bureaucratic inefficiencies, weak governance, and limited access to finance and infrastructure hindered the emergence of a dynamic private sector, mirroring challenges faced by many transition economies. These structural constraints stifled innovation and business sophistication.

Libya also struggled to attract foreign direct investment (FDI) due to a poor business climate and anti-FDI sentiments and policies. In 2010, the World Bank's Ease of Doing Business Index ranked Libya 154th out of 183 countries, reflecting deep-rooted barriers even before the conflict.

The conflict exacerbated these challenges introducing new hurdles for Libya's private sector. According to a United Nations (UN) report, the absence of a conducive business environment, coupled with limited support mechanisms and insufficient incentives, continues to hinder the growth of Libya's private sector and constrain the country's broader economic potential (UN, 2021[2]). The World Bank estimates a 30% decline in foreign direct investment inflows into Libya in the years immediately following the onset of the conflict (World Bank, 2021[1]). Macro-economic uncertainty, political instability, corruption, regulatory policy ambiguity, and poor infrastructure, already prevalent, were further compounded by the conflict.

Despite these challenges, Libya's private sector has shown remarkable resilience. Optimism about a post-conflict recovery persists, with 65% of businesses expressing confidence in the future economic environment, and the number of registered businesses increasing by 15% despite ongoing instability (World Bank, 2021[1]). Stakeholders articulate a long-term goal of economic diversification, aiming to develop higher added-value industries within the hydrocarbons sector and foster new sectors to reduce reliance on oil revenues.

The path to recovery and transformation is intertwined, necessitating short-term measures, such as securing oil production and rendering operational the financial sector, aligned with long-term goals concerning macroeconomic stability, and the development of the private sector. The World Bank reported that Libya's reconstruction needs were estimated at USD 90 billion, providing a substantial opportunity for private sector involvement (World Bank, 2021[1]). Immediate recovery efforts should strategically contribute to the overarching vision of economic diversification. Reconstruction projects, for instance, can be leveraged to develop local industries, but this requires supportive public procurement policies, capacity-building programs, and adequate staffing to ensure local firms can capitalise on these opportunities.

In this context, the "EU-OECD Project on Promoting Public-Private Dialogue in Libya (2020–2023)" was launched to support Libya's post-conflict transition through a participatory, sector-focused dialogue process. The project aimed to improve the business climate by creating spaces for structured engagement between public institutions and private sector actors across Libya's diverse regions. Rooted in the OECD's methodology on Public-Private Dialogue (PPD), the initiative brought together over 200 stakeholders from government, business, and civil society to identify policy challenges, co-create solutions, and strengthen institutional and human capacities at both national and local levels.

This PPD initiative builds on previous OECD work under the MENA Transition Fund project on SME Development in Libya. That project involved sectoral analysis and consultations with public and private actors to assess Libya's economic potential and advance private sector growth. A comprehensive review of sector trends and competitiveness resulted in the OECD publication "SMEs in Libya's Reconstruction", which assessed strategies to diversify the resource-based national economy and examined sectoral GDP contribution, employment, labour productivity, exports, and foreign direct investment (FDI) attractiveness (OECD, 2016[3]). The analysis also considered alignment with Libya's development goals and job creation impact.

To operationalise this approach, the project conducted extensive consultations to identify and prioritise five key economic sectors that offer strategic potential for Libya's economic diversification and resilience: **Banking and Financial Services, Agribusiness, Information and Communication Technology (ICT), Infrastructure and Construction, and Transport and Logistics**. These sectors were selected based on their alignment with Libya's development priorities, their potential for job creation and private investment, and the feasibility of reform efforts given institutional and market realities.

The public-private dialogue process supported by this project not only aimed to generate targeted policy recommendations for each of these sectors but also to build trust, promote inclusive policymaking, and create a foundation for sustainable dialogue mechanisms in the future. The insights and proposals developed through the PPDs reflect the aspirations of Libyan stakeholders and draw on OECD good practices to support implementation.

This report builds on these dialogues and offers a comprehensive overview of Libya's economic context, sectoral challenges, and reform opportunities. It begins with an outline of the national economic landscape, followed by five in-depth sectoral chapters. Each sectoral section combines analytical insights, policy challenges, and stakeholder priorities emerging from the PPD sessions. The report concludes with a synthesis of cross-cutting findings and implementation considerations to inform future policy efforts and donor coordination.

2 Promoting Public Private Dialogue (PPD) in Libya

Introduction

In a context of ongoing fragility, fostering structured dialogue between the public and private sectors in Libya presents both urgent needs and significant challenges. Since 2020, the "Promoting Public-Private Dialogue in Libya" project has worked to lay the foundations for more inclusive, sustained engagement between government institutions and private sector actors. Operating in a post-conflict environment marked by limited state capacity, the project draws on international principles – such as the Kampala Principles on Effective Private Sector Engagement in Development Co-operation (2019) – to promote trust-building, joint problem-solving, and shared ownership of reform processes.

Public-Private Dialogue (PPD) refers to structured, institutionalised processes that bring together public and private stakeholders to identify constraints, co-create policy solutions, and support implementation (Box 2.1). In Libya, the project has used this approach to help surface key policy and regulatory challenges, introduce international experiences relevant to recovery and diversification, and build local familiarity with structured dialogue. Efforts have been made to expand participation beyond Tripoli, engaging regional and sectoral representatives in five key areas: agribusiness, banking and finance, ICT, infrastructure and construction, and transport and logistics. Dialogue has been supported through in-person consultations and a dedicated online platform offering learning resources and analytical tools. While PPD is not a substitute for strong institutions, in fragile settings like Libya it can provide a practical entry point for more inclusive policymaking and long-term resilience.

Box 2.1. PPD as a Tool for Economic Diversification and Private Sector Development

Public-Private Dialogue (PPD) helps address two major barriers to reform in fragile and transitioning economies: information asymmetry and fragmented policymaking. By convening diverse stakeholders, PPD aligns government priorities with private sector needs, grounding policy in market realities and supporting implementation through broader buy-in. It is particularly relevant in contexts focused on economic diversification. In centralised or resource-based economies like Libya, the private sector often lacks voice in policymaking. PPD can promote investment beyond dominant sectors (e.g. oil and gas), encourage competitive markets, and strengthen capacities in both public institutions and business communities.

When well-designed, PPD supports regulatory reform, SME development, sector coordination, and addresses constraints in finance, infrastructure, and labour, contributing to inclusive growth. However, it is not without risks – especially in fragile settings. These include rent-seeking, policy capture, marginalisation of SMEs and regions, or ineffective dialogues with no concrete outcomes (OECD, 2007[4]). PPDs may also become politicised or weaken public accountability if private interests dominate. To succeed, they must be transparent, inclusive, and guided by clear goals and accountability mechanisms. The OECD actively works to mitigate these risks and enhance the effectiveness of PPDs.

Beyond economic outputs, one of the most transformative aspects of PPD is its capacity to foster trust between public institutions and private actors. In post-conflict settings where institutions have weakened legitimacy and businesses operate in uncertainty, the lack of trust can be a major barrier to cooperation. PPD provides a neutral, transparent, and rules-based forum for dialogue, where actors can engage on equal footing. Over time, these structured exchanges help repair institutional relationships, reduce perceptions of arbitrariness in policymaking, and create momentum for sustained engagement. Key features of effective PPDs—such as the presence of impartial facilitators, inclusive stakeholder representation, and clearly defined objectives—contribute to establishing a culture of dialogue. This is essential not only for policy design, but for fostering long-term partnerships that extend beyond the dialogue itself.

The OECD PPD methodology, and the focus on fragile and conflict-affected contexts

The OECD has developed a structured approach to designing, implementing, and sustaining PPDs. This methodology is grounded in international best practices and adapted to the realities of the MENA region. It follows a three-phase process:

- Preparation – Mapping of stakeholders, identification of priority sectors or issues, and development of governance structures and facilitation mechanisms.
- Implementation – Organisation of structured and inclusive consultations, use of evidence-based policy papers to guide discussion, and facilitation of consensus-building across actors.
- Monitoring and Evaluation – Tracking outputs and outcomes, capturing lessons learned, and institutionalising mechanisms for dialogue and accountability.

PPD success depends on local ownership, continuity, and political commitment. The OECD approach emphasises the importance of "champions" within institutions and business communities who can drive the process forward, maintain trust, and ensure that dialogue leads to real policy changes.

The value of PPD is particularly acute in fragile settings, where political instability, institutional fragmentation, and low trust present serious obstacles to reform. In such environments, PPD plays a role in peacebuilding, establishing multi-stakeholder dialogue and collective action. Trust deficits and government instability hinder formal discussions, making it essential to involve technical-level officials and leverage informal communication channels for structured engagement offers a rare opportunity. In particular, PPD offers an opportunity to: i) Bridge public-private divides in contexts of weak formal coordination; ii) Build local ownership over reform by including actors from diverse regions and sectors; iii) Promote inclusive governance by amplifying the voices of SMEs, youth, and women entrepreneurs; iv) Deliver early wins through achievable, non-political policy changes, even when legislative progress is limited.

For these reasons, the OECD's work in Libya and other fragile states has focused on tailoring the PPD process to the context—prioritising local implementation partners, decentralised dialogue formats, and realistic, consensus-based reform agendas. In Libya, this approach has helped restore channels of communication between public authorities and economic actors across regions, enabling the co-design of policy solutions in key sectors such as finance, agribusiness, ICT, infrastructure, and transport

Since its inception, the "Promoting Public-Private Dialogue in Libya" project has undertaken a range of targeted activities to foster inclusive engagement and build the foundations for structured dialogue. Over 200 representatives from both the public and private sectors have been directly involved in consultations, workshops, and exchanges to identify priorities areas for the project. Benefitting from the support of a local implementing partner, the project has mapped and developed sector-specific networks across five key sectors – agribusiness, banking and finance, ICT, infrastructure and construction, and transport and logistics – spanning four different regions of the country. This groundwork has enabled more tailored and regionally responsive engagement with key stakeholders.

To support learning and capacity-building, the project has delivered 45 PPD sessions and workshops, offering a platform for dialogue on public-private collaboration as a pathway to economic growth and diversification. Peer-learning sessions have helped reinforce national dialogue and build bridges to international experience, while policy recommendations and reform initiatives have been refined through targeted exchanges with regional practitioners. Feedback from Libyan stakeholders and donor partners underscored the project's relevance and effectiveness, with many viewing it as a strong foundation for sustainable economic recovery and a broader political transition.

PPD as a tool for resilient policymaking, in regional Libya

Successful Public-Private Dialogue (PPD) hinges on inclusivity, a nuanced understanding of local power dynamics, and the presence of well-connected local facilitators who can build trust and ensure long-term sustainability. In fragile contexts, a persistent challenge lies in reaching and mobilising marginalised groups, particularly those in remote or geographically isolated areas.

Libya's deep regional disparities present distinct obstacles to effective PPD. In the Northwest, cities such as Misrata, Zintan, and Zawiya benefit from relatively developed local structures, yet are undermined by internal tensions, smuggling networks, and human trafficking, which erode governance and security. The Northeast – home to Benghazi, Bayda, Tobruk, and Derna – has comparatively stronger institutions, shaped by early support for the 2011 uprising and the NATO intervention. However, the region remains vulnerable to instability due to ongoing factional rivalries and movements advocating for regional autonomy. In the South, governance is more heavily influenced by ethnic and tribal affiliations, with chronic challenges related to border control, oil infrastructure, and systemic marginalisation. These dynamics heighten the region's susceptibility to conflict and hinder inclusive policy engagement (Fitzgerald, 2018[5]). To account for these differences, different PPD sessions were held in: Tripoli, Benghazi, Misrata, and Sabha.

Libya's regional differences also reflect varying degrees of fragility. In the Northwest, cities like Misrata, Zintan, and

- Tripoli: Libya's capital faces political fragmentation, security challenges, and economic instability due to corruption, a liquidity crisis, and power outages. PPD discussions prioritised restoring trust in banking, expanding credit access for SMEs, and enhancing anti-money laundering measures. Policymakers also explored ways to reduce ICT costs, digitalise public services, and improve infrastructure financing through public-private partnerships (PPPs) to reactivate stalled projects.
- Benghazi: Conflict has severely impacted Benghazi's economy, with infrastructure damage and limited investment. While port and airport reopenings offer hope, youth unemployment remains high. PPD discussions focused on agriculture sector transformation, advocating for regulatory reforms, stakeholder collaboration, and technology adoption. Banking sector dialogues supported governance reforms, anti-money laundering laws, and a Credit Guarantee Fund for micro- small- and medium-sized enterprises (MSMEs). Stakeholders also explored enhancing telecommunications infrastructure through PPPs and streamlined regulations.
- Misrata: Considered more stable, Misrata's economy benefits from its port, airport, and state enterprises. PPD discussions addressed transportation improvements, advocating for better road safety, logistics integration, and airport/port operations. A proposal for a unified transportation strategy was developed. In agriculture, policymakers emphasised education, food safety, and resource management, introducing initiatives such as awareness campaigns, a safe food initiative, and modern irrigation practices.

- Sebha: A key logistical hub in southern Libya, Sebha struggles with high unemployment, informal economies, and weak infrastructure. PPD discussions explored infrastructure financing and governance, promoting legal reforms, PPPs, and digital governance. In ICT, policymakers considered regional sub-data centres, fibre-optic expansion, and private sector incentives. The agricultural sector dialogue addressed legislative updates, public-private collaboration, and activating free trade zones for investment and job creation.

The PPD Project in Libya successfully conducted 45 targeted sessions in these four cities, assessing key challenges and opportunities in each sector. These efforts were complemented by capacity-building activities and peer-learning exchanges to strengthen knowledge-sharing and engagement with regional stakeholders. To ensure continuity, a technical steering committee was established. The analysis in the following chapters provides a comprehensive overview of discussions, with final recommendations reflecting key takeaways from the PPD sessions.

Successful Public-Private Dialogue (PPD) depends on inclusivity, a deep understanding of local power dynamics, and the involvement of well-connected local facilitators who can build trust and promote long-term sustainability. In fragile settings like Libya, mobilising marginalised groups—particularly in geographically remote or underserved areas—remains a persistent challenge. These difficulties are compounded by political instability, institutional fragmentation, and stark regional disparities that affect the capacity for effective policy dialogue.

Libya's regional landscape is marked by distinct governance structures and varying degrees of fragility, each posing different challenges for implementing PPD. In the Northwest, cities such as Misrata, Zintan, and Zawiya benefit from relatively developed local institutions, but face persistent issues such as internal political tensions, smuggling, and human trafficking, all of which erode governance and undermine security. In the Northeast, including Benghazi, Bayda, Tobruk, and Derna, stronger local institutions emerged early on due to support for the 2011 uprising and the NATO intervention. However, this region is still affected by factional rivalries and movements advocating for regional autonomy, threatening long-term stability. In the South, governance is shaped by ethnic and tribal affiliations, with deep-rooted challenges linked to border control, oil infrastructure, and marginalisation. These factors increase the region's vulnerability to conflict and limit its integration into national policy processes (Fitzgerald, 2018[5]).

To respond to these regional differences, the PPD project implemented a decentralised engagement strategy, organising structured dialogue sessions in Tripoli, Benghazi, Misrata, and Sebha. These sessions were tailored to the specific economic and governance challenges of each locality:

- In Tripoli, the capital's political fragmentation, liquidity crisis, and power outages created a difficult environment for business. PPD discussions prioritised rebuilding trust in the banking sector, expanding credit access for SMEs, and strengthening anti-money laundering measures. Policymakers also explored strategies to lower ICT costs, digitalise public services, and unlock infrastructure financing through public-private partnerships (PPPs) to reactivate stalled projects.
- In Benghazi, a city heavily affected by conflict, infrastructure damage and limited investment continue to constrain growth. While recent reopenings of the port and airport are promising, youth unemployment remains high. PPD dialogues focused on modernising the agriculture sector through regulatory reform, stakeholder collaboration, and technology adoption. In parallel, the banking dialogue addressed governance reform and the establishment of a Credit Guarantee Fund for MSMEs. Telecommunications infrastructure was also highlighted, with emphasis on PPPs and streamlined regulatory frameworks.

- Misrata, often regarded as one of Libya's more stable cities, benefits from strong commercial infrastructure including a functioning port, airport, and several state enterprises. PPD activities centred on improving transportation, with proposals to enhance road safety, logistics integration, and port/airport operations. A unified national transportation strategy was drafted. In agriculture, emphasis was placed on food safety, environmental sustainability, and educational initiatives, including awareness campaigns and support for modern irrigation techniques.
- In Sebha, a critical logistics hub in the South, the dialogue focused on overcoming widespread unemployment, weak infrastructure, and reliance on informal economies. PPD sessions addressed legal reforms and infrastructure financing, alongside opportunities for digital governance and PPPs. ICT discussions included proposals for regional sub-data centres, fibre-optic expansion, and incentives for private sector investment. In the agriculture sector, the dialogue promoted updated legislation, public-private collaboration, and activation of free trade zones to stimulate investment and job creation.

Through these targeted regional dialogues, the PPD project engaged over 200 stakeholders from across the public and private sectors, helping identify priority areas likely to have a positive impact on different local economies. Supported by a local implementing partner, the project developed sectoral networks across four regions and five strategic sectors. In total, 45 PPD sessions and workshops were delivered, complemented by peer-learning activities and international exchanges. These efforts were supported by a technical steering committee to ensure continuity and alignment. The following section provides details about the sectors and actions identified through the PPD.

Prioritised economic sectors

Building on the insights gathered through regional consultations, the EU-OECD project on *Promoting Public-Private Dialogue in Libya (2020–2023)* identified five strategic sectors as entry points for reform: agribusiness, banking and finance, ICT, infrastructure and construction, and transport and logistics. These sectors were selected based on national development priorities, Libya's economic potential, and the need to foster private sector growth and reduce dependency on public employment. The selection process drew on prior OECD analysis (OECD, 2016[3]), ongoing engagement with Libyan stakeholders, and alignment with regional economic contexts (Box 2.1).

The prioritisation reflects a focus on sectors with strong employment potential, opportunities for value addition and export growth, and relevance to both short-term recovery and longer-term diversification. These findings were reinforced during the development of the *Libya Short-Term Action Plan for SME Development (2020)*, which engaged over 200 public and private institutions across the country. Establishing a national PPD platform around these five sectors has provided a structured space for dialogue, helping to connect local insights with national reform efforts and paving the way for more coherent and inclusive policy implementation.

3 Five strategic sectors as entry points for reform

Introduction

The following section offers a deeper dive into the five strategic sectors identified through the Public-Private Dialogue process. It explores not only the rationale behind their selection, but also the broader economic, institutional, and policy factors that shape their development potential. This analysis aims to shed light on the role these sectors can play in supporting sustainable and inclusive growth in Libya, particularly through job creation, private sector revitalisation, and economic diversification.

In addition to insights gathered directly through the PPD, the section draws on complementary sources of information to provide a more comprehensive understanding of each sector's strengths, challenges, and opportunities. These additional perspectives help to contextualise the sectors within Libya's wider economic landscape and highlight critical enablers — such as infrastructure, finance, or human capital — that can support their transformation. Together, this expanded analysis helps lay the groundwork for more informed, targeted, and coherent sectoral

Banking

The Libyan banking sector plays a critical role in financing investments across key economic sectors, supporting the country's long-term goals of sustainable and inclusive development. However, the sector remains underdeveloped and faces structural challenges, including limited credit access, governance inefficiencies, and the dominance of state-owned banks. Despite these issues, it has significant potential for reform, particularly in promoting financial inclusion, improving transparency, and enhancing financial system resilience.

With over 70% of assets concentrated in a few banks, notably Jumhouria and the National Commercial Bank, Libya's banking sector suffers from limited competition, stifling innovation and restricting credit to the private sector, just 12% of GDP in 2022, one of the lowest levels globally ((IMF, 2023[6]); (World Bank, 2023[7])). Modernisation, particularly through FinTech, could increase financial access and transparency. Expanding digital financial services, such as mobile banking and electronic payments, could also improve data collection for policy design and economic planning (IMF, 2023[8]).

Strengthening anti-money laundering (AML) frameworks is crucial for restoring international confidence. Regulatory gaps have enabled criminal activities, exacerbating the informal economy, and discouraging foreign direct investment (FDI). A robust AML system, aligned with international standards, would enhance the sector's credibility and global integration (IMF, 2023[8]). Both the OECD (2016) and the World Bank (2020) have highlighted Libya's potential to attract FDI if governance, transparency, and financial reforms are prioritised (Rahman and Di Maio, 2020[9]).

Context and Overview

The ongoing crisis within the Central Bank of Libya (CBL) has severely hindered monetary and fiscal policy management since the conflict erupted in 2014. Although recently reunified, the CBL continues to struggle with governance challenges that complicate banking system supervision. Uncoordinated actions in past years, including independent currency issuance by the Eastern branch, have exacerbated instability, affecting liquidity management and financial oversight (IMF, 2023[8]). Despite majority ownership of public banks—holding 90% of deposits and loans—the CBL lacks the capacity to ensure sound credit decisions across the sector (World Bank, 2023[7]).

The crisis has heightened concerns about financial stability. While the CBL now operates under a single leadership, liquidity pressures persist, especially in the western region, where banks rely on Tripoli for foreign exchange transactions. Meanwhile, financial imbalances remain, with some institutions maintaining elevated settlement balances independent of central oversight (IMF, 2023[8]). These challenges complicate monetary policy and reinforce Libya's economic fragmentation.

Libya's commercial banking sector also reflects political and economic instability. Despite liberalisation efforts in the late 2000s that allowed private commercial banks, they held just 10% of total deposits in 2017. Public banks remain closely tied to state-owned enterprises, prioritising lending to state firms and limiting private sector financing (World Bank, 2023[7]).

Table 3.1. List of commercial banks in Libya in 2023

Type of Ownership/Bank	Location
State owned	
Jumhouria Bank	Tripoli
Libyan Foreign Bank	Tripoli
National Commercial Bank	Al-Baidha
Mixed ownership	
North Africa Bank	Tripoli
Sahara Bank BNP Paribas Group	Tripoli
Wahda Bank	Benghazi
Private ownership	
Al Waha Bank	Tripoli
Alejma'a Alarabi Bank	Benghazi
Aman Bank for Commerce and Investment	Tripoli
Al Yaqin Bank	Tripoli
Arab Commercial Bank	Tripoli
Assaray Bank Trade & Investment Bank	Tripoli
Bank of Commerce & Development	Benghazi
Development Bank	Tripoli
First Gulf Libyan Bank	Tripoli
Libyan Islamic Bank	Tripoli
Mediterranean Bank	Benghazi
Nuran Bank	Tripoli
United Bank for Commerce & Investment	Tripoli
Wafa Bank	Tripoli

Source: World Bank 2023, using CBL official data

The underdevelopment of private sector banking has contributed to a decline in financial intermediation activities, particularly since the onset of the conflict (Figure 3.1). The share of value added by the financial sector, as a percentage of GDP, has been shrinking steadily. Despite these challenges, there is cautious optimism about the sector's potential. The CBL forecasts a gradual recovery in credit, particularly for housing, social loans, and loans to non-financial corporations, including small and medium-sized enterprises (SMEs). In 2021, loans to non-financial corporations accounted for over LYD 12 billion (approx. USD 2.71 billion), while social loans saw a significant increase from their historical lows in 2019 (CBL, 2021[10])(Figure 3.2).

Figure 3.1. Financial intermediation activities have declined since the onset of the conflict and the division of the CBL

Value added, % of GDP

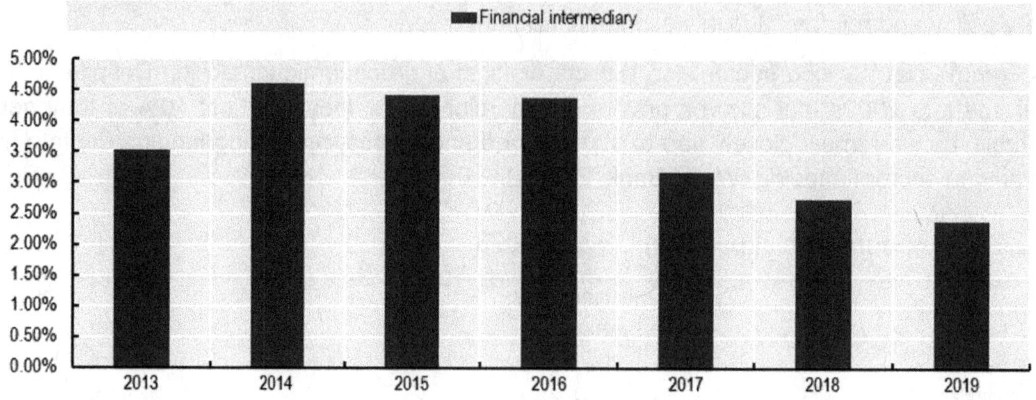

Source: Central Bank of Libya 4th Quarter Economic Bulletin (2021), OECD calculations.

Figure 3.2. Commercial banks credits have increased as stability returned and the dinar was devaluated in 2021

Millions of LYD

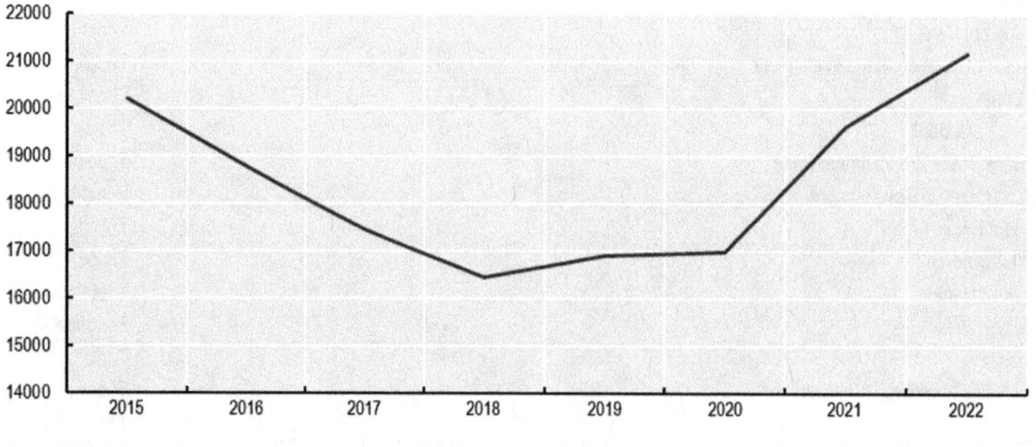

Note: Data from 2022 is from the Central Bank of Libya 2nd Quarter Economic Bulleting, 2022.
Source: Central Bank of Libya 4th Quarter Economic Bulleting, 2021

Libya's domestic credit to the private sector, standing at 17% of GDP in 2020, remains significantly lower than in neighbouring countries such as Tunisia (68%), Jordan (83%), and Morocco (70%), as well as the regional average of 56% (World Bank, 2023[7]) (Figure 3.3). These figures highlight the stark challenges facing the financial sector in providing adequate credit to stimulate economic growth, particularly for the private sector, which is critical for diversification beyond the hydrocarbon sector.

Despite the current instability, Libya's banking sector remains a key area with potential for reform. The development of robust private sector banking and the promotion of financial inclusion could lead to increased financial stability and economic resilience. Strengthening institutional capacity, fostering competition, and enhancing regulatory oversight are essential steps in creating a more inclusive and dynamic banking system.

Figure 3.3. Commercial banks credit given to private sector falls lower than regional peers

Value added, % of GDP

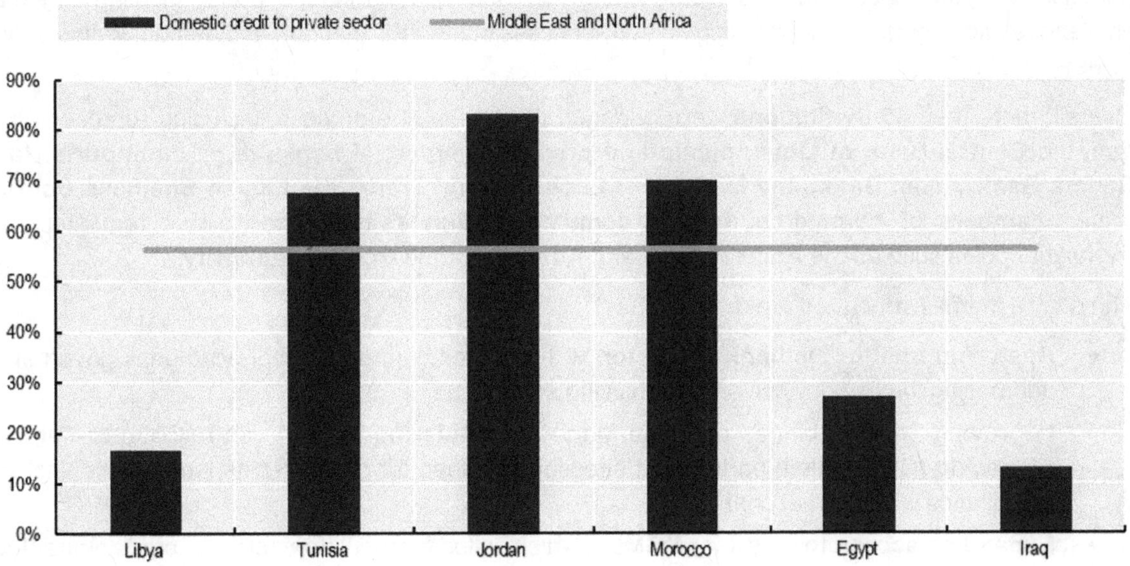

Source: World Bank (2019).

Box 3.1. Public-Private Dialogue Process in the Banking Sector

The Public-Private Dialogue (PPD) for the banking sector was a central pillar of the EU-OECD Project on Promoting Public-Private Dialogue in Libya. Aimed at improving coordination between government and business stakeholders, the PPD focused on restoring confidence in the financial system, enhancing regulatory performance, and advancing inclusive access to finance. A total of **nine sessions** were held between **August 2022 and May 2023**, covering **Tripoli, Benghazi, Sebha, and Misrata**, culminating in a national-level dialogue in Tunis.

The format followed a three-stage dialogue model. First, separate sessions were convened with private and public sector stakeholders to identify key challenges and reform priorities from their respective standpoints. These initial sessions enabled each group to freely explore issues such as liquidity shortages, regulatory bottlenecks, and access to finance, which helped surface recurring themes and build a thematic foundation for dialogue. The final joint session served to validate and consolidate these priorities, with the most notable outcome being that both sectors independently highlighted similar challenges and opportunities—marking an early success of the PPD platform and demonstrating shared ownership of reform pathways.

Overall, more than **35 institutions** were engaged throughout the process, including representatives from the **Central Bank of Libya, public and private commercial banks (e.g., Jumhouria Bank, Sahara Bank, Aman Bank), the Ministry of Economy and Trade, the Libyan Business Council, local chambers of commerce, fintech companies, universities,** and various regulatory and oversight bodies such as the **Audit Bureau** and **Administrative Control Authority**.

Three core themes structured the discussions:

- **Restoring trust in the banking sector**, with debates centred on improving bank governance, addressing the liquidity crisis, and digitising services.
- **Improving performance on Anti-Money Laundering (AML) and Counter-Terrorist Financing (CFT)**, where participants stressed the need for greater transparency, training, and compliance with international standards.
- **Expanding access to credit for MSMEs**, which called for regulatory reforms, credit guarantees, and better coordination between banks and national SME programmes.

The joint sessions resulted in concrete initiatives for each theme. For example, the banking sector committed to digitisation and greater transparency to enhance trust; oversight bodies were tasked with improving compliance with AML/CFT frameworks; and new mechanisms were proposed to support SME financing, including the establishment of a digital platform to connect project owners with funders.

Detailed Analysis of Sector Challenges

Libya's banking sector faces significant challenges that hinder economic development and financial stability. These stem from political instability, institutional inefficiencies, outdated regulations, and the past fragmentation of the Central Bank of Libya (CBL). These issues weaken credit provision and limit the sector's role in economic recovery.

CBL Fragmentation and Structural Imbalances

Since 2014, the CBL split has severely undermined monetary policy, liquidity, and foreign exchange management. Uncoordinated currency printing and loan issuance have fuelled inflation and eroded trust in the financial system (IMF, 2023[8]). The Eastern branch's inability to issue US dollars has caused liquidity constraints in the west, while it continues to hold large settlement balances, further destabilising the system (IMF, 2023[21]). The current situation is still unstable and generates large transaction costs for the national economy.

Weak Regulation and Governance

Libya's outdated regulatory framework limits effective banking oversight. The CBL's dual role as regulator and majority shareholder in major banks like Jumhouria creates conflicts of interest, undermining governance, competition, and innovation (IMF, 2023[8]). Public banks dominate, while private banks hold just 10% of deposits (World Bank, 2023[7]).

Additionally, the 2013 ban on interest-based lending forced banks to transition to Islamic finance, slowing financial product development. A lack of expertise and regulatory oversight has further delayed progress (IMF, 2023[8]).

Limited Credit and High Non-Performing Loans

Libya's private sector credit remains at just 17% of GDP—well below the regional average of 56% and countries like Tunisia (68%) and Jordan (83%) (World Bank, 2023[7]). State-owned banks prioritise lending to SOEs over SMEs, while weak underwriting and risk management worsen capital allocation inefficiencies (IMF, 2023[8]).

Non-performing loans (NPLs) remain high at around 20% since 2011 (IMF, 2023[8]). Weak asset classification and provisioning practices understate the issue, overstating capital adequacy under Basel I. Without accurate data, policymakers struggle to design effective financial sector reforms.

Financial Inclusion and Digitalisation

Financial inclusion remains a major challenge in Libya, especially in rural areas where access to formal financial services is limited. While the country performs relatively well in terms of account ownership and use of internet-based financial services when compared with peers (Figure 3.4), only a small fraction of the population has access to basic banking services like savings accounts, credit, and electronic payments (World Bank, 2023[7]). The absence of a widespread digital banking infrastructure further restricts participation in the formal economy.

FinTech solutions could enhance financial inclusion, particularly in underserved regions. However, Libya's regulatory framework has yet to support digital financial services. Without the necessary infrastructure and legal backing, the benefits of digitalisation—such as better credit access and greater transparency—will remain unrealised (IMF, 2023[8]).

Figure 3.4. Libya's financial inclusion performs comparatively well in the region

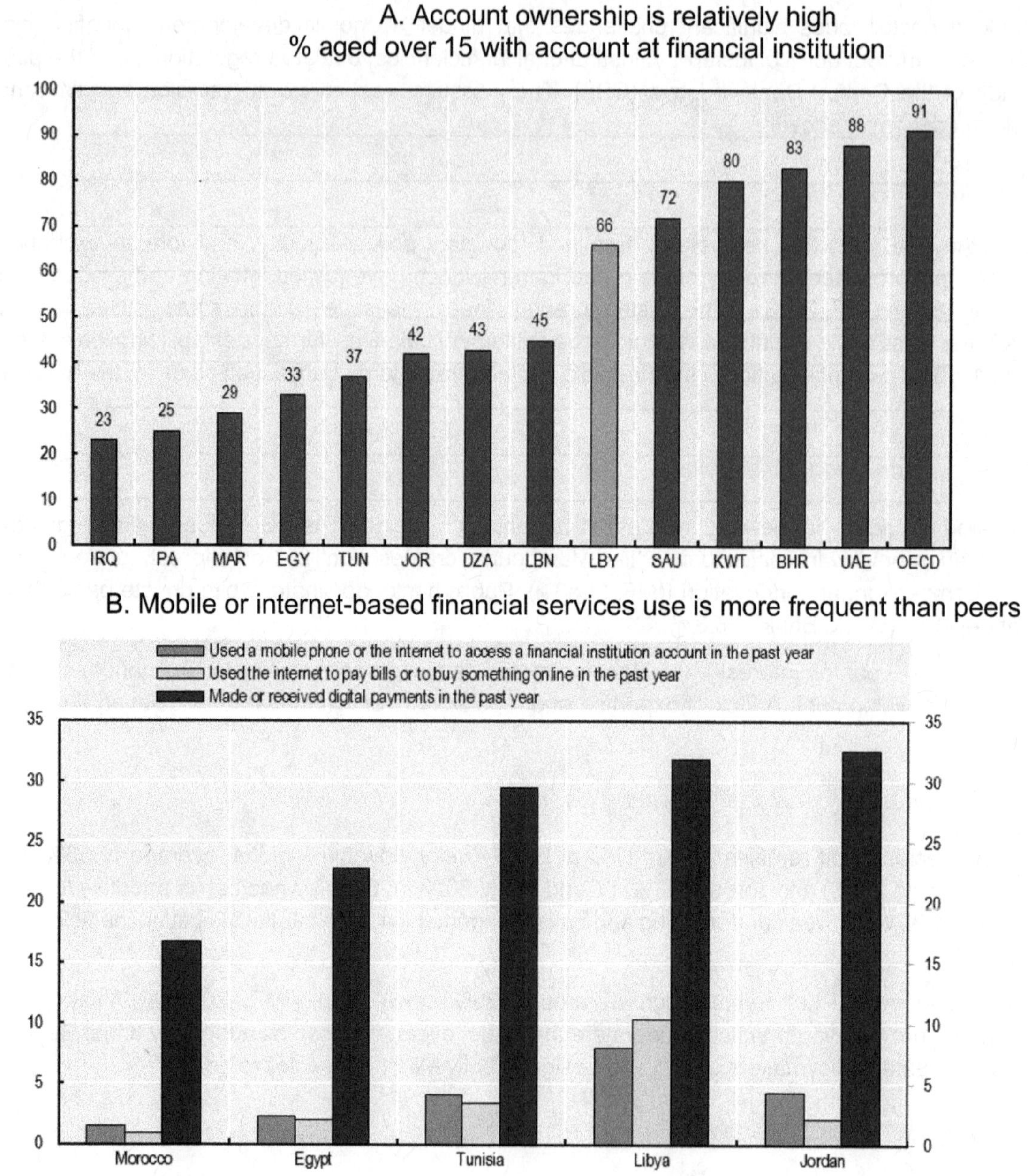

Source: World Bank Global Findex database (2017).

Anti-Money Laundering and Combating the Financing of Terrorism (AML/CFT) Deficiencies

Libya's banking sector is highly vulnerable to financial crime due to weak oversight and institutional gaps. The Central Bank's lack of a robust anti-money laundering (AML) framework and limited resources at the Financial Intelligence Unit (FIU) have fuelled illicit financial activities (IMF, 2023[8]). In 2022, banks filed alarmingly few suspicious activity reports (SARs), reflecting inadequate monitoring and controls (IMF, 2023[8]).

These AML/CFT deficiencies not only expose the sector to crime but also erode international confidence, further isolating Libya from the global financial system. Strengthening AML regulations and enhancing FIU capacity are critical for restoring credibility and attracting foreign investment.

Political Instability and Security Risks

Political instability and conflict continue to threaten Libya's banking sector. The divided political landscape has stalled financial sector reforms, while ongoing conflict disrupts economic activity and weakens financial institutions. Banks face heightened risks, including physical damage in conflict zones and increased fraud and cyber threats in a fragile security environment (World Bank, 2023[7]).

Strategic Priorities and Policy Recommendations

Reforming the Libyan banking sector requires a multi-pronged approach that tackles the deep-rooted structural issues while leveraging the sector's potential to contribute to economic recovery and development. This section outlines key policy priorities that align with OECD best practices, focusing on liquidity, governance, financial inclusion, anti-money laundering, and access to credit, with an emphasis on Libya's unique challenges.

Policy Priority 1: Restoring Trust and Reputation to the Libyan Banking Sector

I. Increase Liquidity in the Banking Sector

Libya's banking sector faces chronic liquidity shortages, eroding public trust and pushing many to rely on informal networks. In 2017, only 17% of Libyans saved at a formal financial institution, while 44% borrowed informally, reflecting a lack of confidence in banks (World Bank, 2017[11]). The 2021 Libyan dinar devaluation temporarily reduced currency held outside banks, but liquidity issues persist. Surveys in 2021 showed 28% of households struggled to access cash due to banking sector constraints (REACH, 2022[12]).

To address this, the Central Bank of Libya (CBL) should improve liquidity management by strengthening interbank markets and introducing short-term liquidity instruments aligned with Islamic finance. Enhancing deposit insurance schemes could also help restore confidence and encourage formal savings.

II. Restore Global Linkages to Strengthen International Trade

Libya's conflict has damaged its international banking reputation, raising concerns over money laundering and terrorism financing. Consequently, many global banks have cut correspondent relationships with Libyan banks, increasing trade costs (World Bank, 2019[13]). Higher Letter of Credit (LC) fees have disproportionately affected Libyan businesses, restricting access to global markets.

To restore confidence, Libya should reassess the CBL's ownership of commercial banks and move toward independent governance, as recommended in the first public-private banking dialogue. Strengthening AML/CFT regulations is also crucial to reconnect Libyan banks to global financial networks and lower trade costs.

III. Diversify Bank Assets and Services

Libyan banks rely heavily on demand deposits, which made up 87% of total deposits in 2018, exposing the sector to cash shortages and instability (World Bank, 2019[13]) Loans and credits accounted for only 18% of bank assets, highlighting the limited financial services available to businesses and individuals. This dependence on short-term deposits restricts banks from financing long-term investments essential for economic growth.

To enhance resilience, banks must diversify their asset portfolios by expanding financial products, including long-term savings, investment options, and SME lending. Reducing reliance on short-term liquidity will strengthen the sector's ability to support economic development.

Policy Priority 2: Improving Libya's Performance in Anti-Money Laundering (AML) Policies

I. Improve the Regulatory Framework for AML/CFT

Restoring trust in Libya's banking sector requires a well-enforced AML/CFT framework. While an AML/CFT law was introduced in 2017, enforcement remains weak. The law created the National Committee for Combating Money Laundering and a Financial Intelligence Unit (FIU), but regulators lack the capacity to enforce penalties and ensure compliance (World Bank, 2019[13]).

Strengthening Libya's AML/CFT system requires bolstering FIU capacity, improving data sharing among regulators, and enhancing monitoring of suspicious activities. The FIU needs more resources to process suspicious activity reports (SARs) and investigate violations, as current backlogs indicate under-resourcing (IMF, 2023[8]). Aligning regulations with Financial Action Task Force (FATF) standards is key to restoring global confidence in Libyan financial institutions.

Policy Priority 3: Improving Access to Credit for MSMEs for an Inclusive Economy

I. Increase Lending to MSMEs

Access to finance remains a major barrier for Libyan businesses, especially MSMEs. In 2020, domestic credit to the private sector was just 16.5% of GDP, far below the 56.4% regional average in 2017 (World Bank, 2023[7]). Limited credit access stifles private sector growth and economic diversification.

To boost MSME lending, Libya must establish targeted credit programs and activate the Credit Guarantee Fund to mitigate lending risks. The CBL should collaborate with banks to develop databases tracking MSME performance, improving credit risk assessment and lending decisions. A data-driven approach will enhance credit allocation and reduce default risks.

II. Establish a Credit Governance Framework

Strengthening credit governance is crucial for improving access to finance and reducing corruption. Clear credit risk appetites, underwriting standards, and exposure limits will enhance lending decisions and mitigate non-performing loan (NPL) risks. Automating credit reporting will improve data accuracy and make the credit registry more effective, ensuring better credit allocation.

A strong credit governance framework will also foster private sector growth, enabling Libyan MSMEs to drive economic expansion and job creation.

III. Support the Growth of FinTech for Financial Inclusion

While financial inclusion in Libya surpasses the MENA average—with 66% of adults holding bank accounts compared to 37% regionally—access to digital financial services remains limited (World Bank, 2017[11]). In 2017, only 8% of Libyans reported using mobile or internet banking, pointing to persistent barriers to FinTech adoption. Nonetheless, the emergence of services such as Mobicash and Idfali demonstrates the growing potential of FinTech to enhance financial inclusion, ease liquidity constraints, and offer more accessible financial tools to both individuals and businesses.

Unlocking this potential will require targeted regulatory reforms, particularly around mobile banking and e-payment systems. The Central Bank of Libya (CBL) could play a catalytic role by streamlining licensing procedures for digital financial service providers, while ensuring robust consumer protection and cybersecurity standards. In parallel, efforts to promote financial literacy—especially among underserved populations and SMEs—will be essential to foster trust and uptake of digital financial services. Additionally, strengthening the internal capacities of financial institutions to evaluate SME proposals and tailor services to their needs is crucial for improving credit access and fostering sustainable enterprise growth. Expanding FinTech, when combined with these enabling measures, can support broader financial inclusion, enhance transparency, and help mitigate risks related to financial crime.

Conclusion and Implementation considerations

Reforming Libya's banking sector is crucial for fostering sustainable and inclusive economic growth. Persistent challenges—liquidity shortages, weak regulatory frameworks, limited credit access, and low financial inclusion—must be tackled through a phased approach to implementation. Drawing on OECD best practices, this paper outlines key priorities, including liquidity management, stronger anti-money laundering (AML) measures, FinTech adoption, and improved credit access for micro, small, and medium enterprises (MSMEs). If implemented effectively, these reforms can transform Libya's banking sector into a catalyst for economic recovery and development.

Short-Term Priorities. Immediate efforts should focus on stabilising liquidity. The Central Bank of Libya (CBL) must introduce short-term liquidity instruments and enhance deposit insurance schemes to protect savings and restore public confidence. Reinforcing AML/CFT frameworks is equally critical; strengthening the Financial Intelligence Unit (FIU) and aligning regulations with Financial Action Task Force (FATF) guidelines will improve financial integrity. Governance reforms at the CBL, including reactivating its board of directors and establishing internal oversight committees, will enhance decision-making and accountability.

Medium-Term Goals. Expanding financial inclusion through FinTech should be a priority. Updating regulations to support mobile banking and digital payments will improve financial access while addressing liquidity challenges. Additionally, increasing lending to MSMEs is essential for economic diversification. Activating the Credit Guarantee Fund and strengthening credit governance will encourage banks to extend loans to small businesses. Establishing an MSME performance database will help assess credit risk, leading to more efficient lending decisions.

Long-Term Vision. To build resilience, Libya's banking sector must diversify its financial offerings. Developing long-term savings accounts, investment products, and specialised financial instruments will reduce reliance on short-term deposits and strengthen banks' ability to finance large-scale development projects essential for sustained growth.

The Broader Impact of Reform. A well-executed phased implementation will yield significant economic benefits. Restoring liquidity will rebuild trust in financial institutions, leading to greater formal savings and increased private-sector lending—particularly to MSMEs, which are vital for job creation and diversification. Strengthening AML/CFT measures will improve Libya's global banking reputation, easing international trade and reducing transaction costs.

Expanding financial inclusion through FinTech will empower more Libyans to engage in the formal economy, reducing poverty and fostering inclusive growth. A more competitive and diversified banking sector will enhance resilience to external shocks, stimulate innovation, and support macroeconomic stability, laying the foundation for long-term prosperity.

By embracing this phased approach to implementation and leveraging global best practices, Libya can transform its banking sector into a robust engine of growth. Strengthening financial institutions will not only drive economic stability and diversification but also pave the way for a more resilient and prosperous future.

Information and Communication Technology (ICT)

Digital transformation presents a major opportunity for Libya's economic diversification and modernisation. ICT adoption can enhance firm productivity, drive innovation, and reduce reliance on the oil sector. Expanding digital public services can also streamline business operations and regulatory compliance, improving efficiency and access to essential services (OECD, 2020[14]). Despite these benefits, Libya's private sector remains largely domestic-focused, with 88% of businesses serving local consumers (World Bank, 2023[7]). The limited use of IT solutions restricts growth and international market access, making digital adoption crucial for competitiveness.

ICT has been recognised as a strategic priority for Libya's private sector. The OECD (2016) highlighted strong demand, low entry barriers in some segments, and infrastructure improvement potential (OECD, 2016[15]). A UNDP labour market assessment projected 50% sector growth within three years, significantly boosting employment (UNDP, 2021[16]). ICT plays a dual role as a direct job creator and as an enabler of broader economic activity through workforce digitalisation and service delivery enhancements. The World Bank also emphasised its importance for attracting young talent and foreign investment, integrating Libya into global value chains, and strengthening economic resilience (Rahman and Di Maio, 2020[9]).

However, digital services, including finance, face structural constraints. Libya's 4G coverage is 67%, well below the MENA average of 82%, while power outages and underdeveloped telecommunications infrastructure further hinder progress (World Bank, 2023[7]). State monopolies in key sectors stifle competition and innovation. Additionally, the absence of legal frameworks on data protection, cybercrime, and consumer rights discourages investment and limits the growth of digital service providers, including financial institutions.

Unlocking the ICT sector's potential requires targeted investments in infrastructure, such as expanding high-speed internet and improving service reliability. Policies that incentivise SMEs to adopt digital technologies and enhance workforce digital skills are equally essential. Strengthening ICT will not only accelerate sectoral growth but also support Libya's broader economic diversification and modernisation efforts.

Context and Overview

Libya's ICT sector offers a strong opportunity for economic diversification and modernisation. Despite political and economic challenges, the sector continues to demonstrate growth potential. According to the International Telecommunication Union (ITU), mobile phone penetration in Libya reached an impressive 90% by 2017, with most of the population owning a mobile device. However, internet usage lagged behind, with only 21.8% of the population accessing the internet at least once over a three-month period (Figure 3.5). This stark digital divide underscores the urgent need for substantial investment in digital infrastructure.

Figure 3.5. Internet usage in Libya has been increasing, but remains low

% of population that accessed the internet at least once in three months

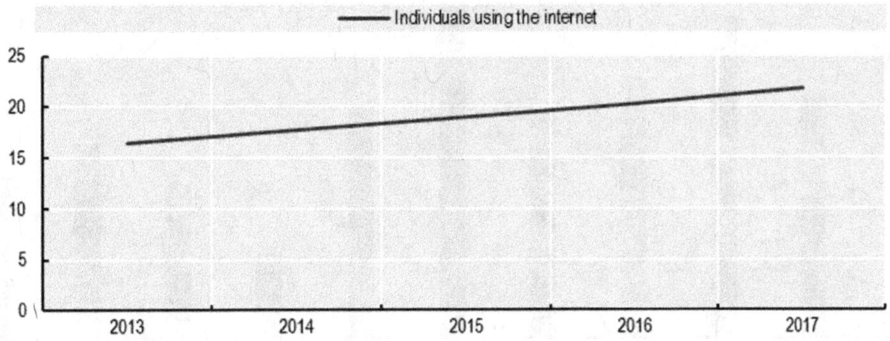

Source: International Telecommunication Union

Libya's ICT sector operates under a mix of government oversight and growing private involvement but remains underdeveloped compared to regional standards. The Ministry of Communications and Informatics sets policy and regulatory standards while driving telecommunications and digital services. Alongside the General Authority for Communications and Informatics, it plays a key role in shaping and implementing ICT initiatives.

Regulation of Libya's ICT sector is complex, hampered by political instability and shifting administrative control. The regulatory framework requires modernisation to support digital transformation, investment, and competition. Weak legal structures on cybersecurity, data protection, and e-commerce further constrain the sector's growth, limiting its contribution to national development.

Despite these challenges, Libya is working to revitalise its ICT sector as part of its economic diversification strategy. Initiatives such as digital governance platforms and workforce digital skills development aim to strengthen infrastructure and regulatory frameworks. These efforts seek to attract investment, foster innovation, and build a resilient digital economy (UNDP, 2021[16]).

The private sector's role in Libya's ICT landscape is expanding but remains small. Local firms and a few foreign entities operate in mobile telephony, internet services, and IT solutions, though state-owned enterprises—particularly Libyana and Almadar—dominate the market. These companies, despite state control, are pursuing innovation and service expansion amid economic and infrastructure challenges (World Bank, 2023[7]).

Digital skills, especially among Libyan youth, are increasingly vital for employment. A 2018 survey found that job seekers and private sector employees consider computer and internet skills crucial for hiring and career advancement (Abughaighis, Tantoush and Hmedan, 2018[17]). This rising emphasis on ICT capabilities reflects the sector's growing importance in the labour market.

Libya's ICT sector also shows economic promise through ICT services exports. In 2016, Libya exported USD 17 million in ICT services, a 66% increase since 2010. Though still modest, this growth signals an emerging capability that could drive broader economic impact (Figure 3.6).

Figure 3.6. Libya is eminently an ICT services importer but its exports have increased in value and share in the last decade

Left axis show Millions of USD Dollars; Right axis show ICT exports share relative to imports

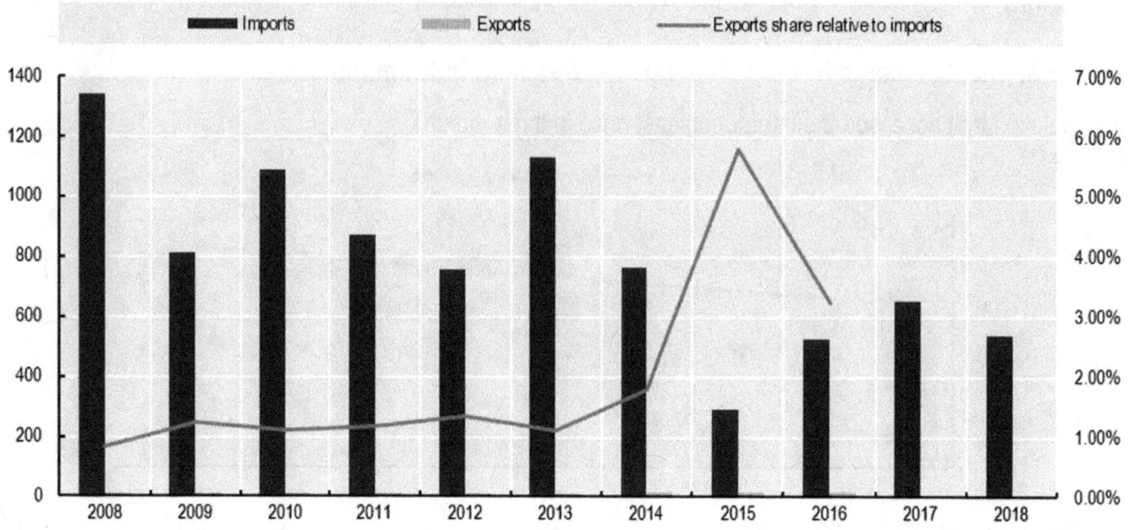

Source: IMF DOTS Data

To leverage the full potential of the ICT sector, Libya needs focused investments in ICT infrastructure, such as expanding high-speed internet access and improving service reliability, especially given the current disparities in 4G coverage and internet speed relative to the MENA region. Additionally, policies to incentivise SMEs to adopt digital technologies and to develop the digital skills of the workforce are essential. These steps will not only enhance the sector's direct contribution to the economy but also support broader national goals of economic diversification and modernisation.

Box 3.2. Public-Private Dialogue Process in the ICT Sector

The Public-Private Dialogue (PPD) process for Libya's ICT sector was conducted under the EU-OECD project as part of a broader effort to promote economic diversification and build sector resilience through inclusive policymaking. The PPD provided a structured platform to bring together key public institutions and private ICT actors to jointly identify barriers to growth and develop actionable reforms.

The ICT PPD process was held across **three Libyan cities—Benghazi (19–22 September 2022), Sebha (13–15 December 2022), and Tripoli (15–17 May 2023)**—in line with the project's commitment to ensuring regional representation. In each city, a **three-stage format** was applied: separate sessions with public and private stakeholders (Private-Private and Public-Public) to capture perspectives on sector-specific challenges, followed by a Joint Session to validate the findings and propose reform initiatives. This structure enabled participants to safely articulate concerns, build consensus, and foster mutual understanding. A final **national session held in Tunis (29–30 November 2023)** brought together key insights from the regional dialogues for consolidation and validation.

Over **70 participants** from more than **35 institutions** took part in these ICT dialogues, including the **Public Telecommunications Authority, Ministry of Economy, Ministry of Planning, National Authority for Information Security and Safety, Libya Post, Tatweer Research, and leading ICT firms and start-ups**. This diverse group ensured that both national policy actors and grassroots innovators were represented.

The dialogues were anchored around **three thematic priorities**:

- **Improving ICT Costs and Infrastructure**: Participants discussed challenges such as outdated infrastructure, fragmented mandates, lack of investment, and bureaucratic inefficiencies. Proposed solutions included the development of a national telecommunications strategy, restructuring public telecom entities, and encouraging shared investment in fibre infrastructure to reduce service costs and increase reach.
- **Developing an Effective Business and Regulatory Environment**: Stakeholders raised concerns about weak legal protections for digital transactions and user data, absence of stakeholder engagement in policymaking, and insufficient support for MSMEs. In response, initiatives focused on improving licensing standards, supporting business incubators, modernising ICT-related curricula, and promoting secure digital ecosystems.
- **Digitalising Public Services**: Public and private actors identified major barriers to e-governance, including lack of interoperability, absence of a unified digital identity framework, and limited public awareness. Solutions focused on creating a national e-governance vision, improving cybersecurity awareness, and introducing an interoperable digital payment gateway.

The joint sessions served as a pivotal moment in each city. They validated the alignment between public and private sector perspectives—demonstrating a shared understanding of core challenges and a readiness to co-develop reforms. Concrete initiatives proposed included the **National Digital Cloud project**, a **national cybersecurity awareness campaign**, and institutional reforms to enhance accountability and efficiency in digital service provision.

Detailed Analysis of Sector Challenges

Infrastructure Deficiencies

Libya's ICT infrastructure lacks the depth and reliability of more developed markets, despite extensive mobile coverage. While 3G coverage stands at 98%, exceeding the MENA average of 93%, 4G availability remains critically low at just 40%, trailing far behind near-universal coverage in Morocco, Egypt, and Tunisia (ITU, 2021[18]). This shortfall underscores the urgent need for investment in next-generation network technologies, including 5G, to strengthen economic activities and expand digital services.

High-speed broadband is essential for businesses to engage in data-intensive operations and adopt advanced digital tools such as cloud computing and big data analytics. However, Libya lags significantly, with average download speeds ranging from 5.3 to 17.2 Mbps, far below Jordan's 17.7 to 109 Mbps. This disparity severely limits the private sector's ability to compete in an increasingly digital global economy.

Figure 3.7. Fixed Broadband Speed in Libya is low compared with the average in the MENA Region

Average experienced download speed of fixed broadband connections (2022)

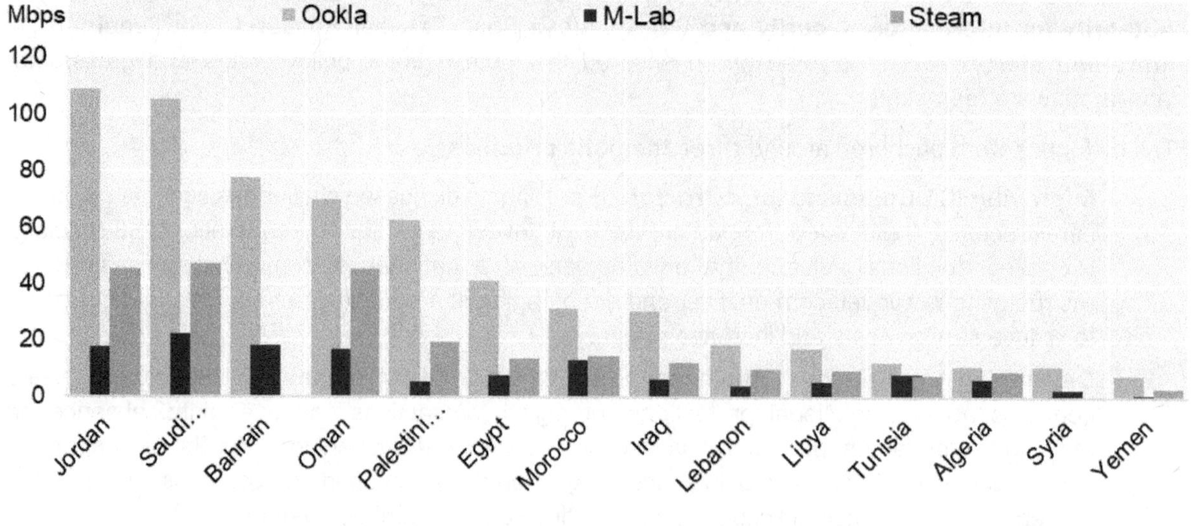

Note: Speedtest (Ookla) data are for July 2022; M-Lab (Worldwide Broadband Speed League) speeds were measured in a 12-month period to 30 June 2022; and Steam data are for September 2022.
Sources: Speedtest (Ookla) [https://www.speedtest.net/global-index], M-Lab (Worldwide broadband speed league) [https://www.cable.co.uk/broadband/speed/worldwide-speed-league/] and Steam [https://store.steampowered.com/stats/content].

High Costs of Internet and Digital Services

The cost of ICT services in Libya remains a critical barrier. In 2021, fixed broadband costs were 4.5% of GNI per capita, substantially higher than in Egypt and Tunisia at 3%, and even Morocco at 4.2% (ITU, 2021[18]). Similarly, mobile broadband costs were 6.2% of GNI per capita, among the highest in the region. These high costs limit accessibility for both individuals and businesses, particularly SMEs, which are crucial for economic diversification.

Regulatory Gaps

Libya's digital economy is constrained by the absence of a comprehensive legal framework covering data protection, online privacy, cybercrime prevention, online consumer protection, and e-signatures. This gap not only places Libya behind its regional counterparts but also creates a risky and uncertain environment for businesses and investors (Global Cybersecurity Index, 2022) (Figure 3.8). Establishing robust legal structures is essential to foster a secure, competitive, and innovative digital market.

Figure 3.8. Libya performs poorly in terms of cybersecurity in comparison to international standards

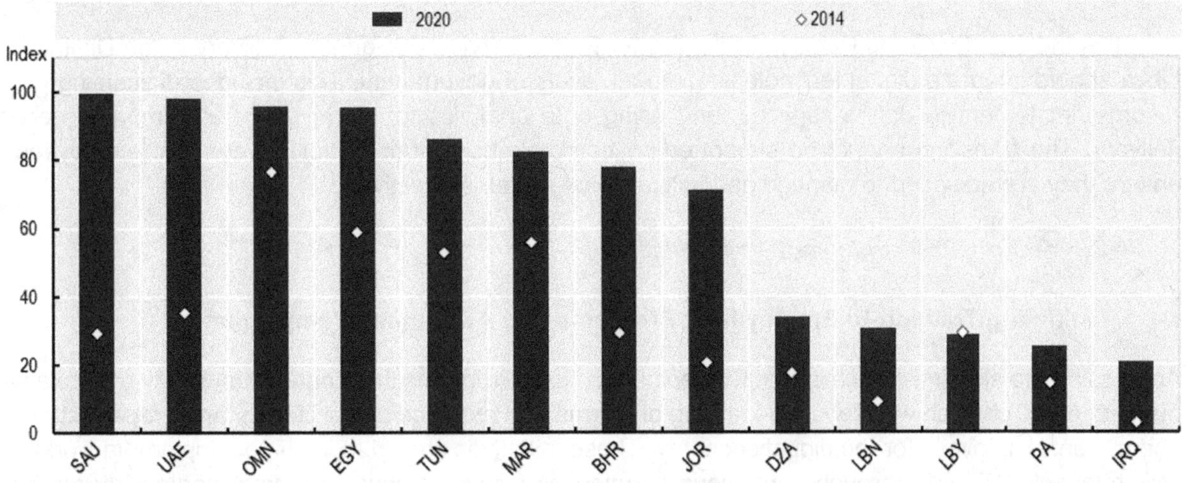

Note: The Global Cybersecurity Index (GCI) is computed on the basis of the following pillars: legal (legal institutions and frameworks dealing with cybersecurity and cybercrime); technical (technical institutions and frameworks dealing with cybersecurity); organisational (policy co-ordination institutions and strategies for cybersecurity development at the national level); capacity building (existence of research and development, education and training programmes, and certified professionals and public sector agencies fostering capacity building) and co-operation (refers to partnerships, co-operative frameworks and information-sharing networks).
Source: ITU (2022), Global Cybersecurity Index, https://www.itu.int/epublications/publication/D-STR-GCI.01-2021-HTM-E

Lack of Digital Skills

The adoption of basic to advanced ICTs is crucial for spurring innovation and enhancing productivity. However, the digital skills gap in Libya, coupled with high costs and regulatory uncertainty, discourages firms from embracing these technologies. Addressing these challenges through targeted training programs, incentives for digital adoption, and partnerships with international tech firms could significantly enhance the sector's growth potential.

Strategic Priorities and Policy Recommendations

Policy Priority 1: Strengthening the ICT sector

Creating an ICT Business Association:

A unified voice for the ICT sector is essential for advocacy and growth. Establishing an industry association, similar to Jordan's Int@j, will facilitate collaboration, advocate for the sector's needs, and strengthen relationships between the private and public sectors. This association will play a crucial role in shaping sectoral policies and ensuring that the sector's potential contribution to the national economy is maximised.

Policy Priority 2: Enhancing Digital Governance and Public Sector Transformation

Launching Digital Governance Initiatives:

Aligned with the General Authority of Communications and Informatics' national strategy, transitioning to digital governance is a strategic priority. This transformation will improve government accountability, efficiency, and transparency, reducing corruption and enhancing public service delivery. Digital governance initiatives will also facilitate easier and more transparent interactions between citizens and the government, promoting greater civic engagement and satisfaction.

Digital Government Transformation:

Adopting the OECD's Good Practice Principles for Public Service Design and Delivery in the Digital Age, Libya should integrate digital technologies into all levels of government. This includes digitalising public records, implementing online services, and using data analytics to inform policy and improve service delivery. The transition should be supported by comprehensive training for government employees to ensure they are equipped to manage and utilise digital systems effectively.

Policy Priority 3: Developing Digital Skills and Talent

Initiating Training-to-Employment Programs and Awareness Campaigns:

Addressing the skills mismatch in the ICT sector is critical. Programs that connect university curricula with market needs, coupled with robust e-learning platforms, will enhance digital literacy and prepare students and current employees for the digital economy. These initiatives should focus on equipping the workforce with relevant ICT skills through continuous learning and development programs, particularly targeting public sector employees to foster a digitally competent government workforce.

Developing Digital Talent in the Public Sector:

Following the OECD Framework for Digital Talent and Skills in the Public Sector, Libya should focus on creating a supportive environment for digital transformation. This includes developing leadership that champions digital initiatives, building a culture of continuous learning and adaptation, and ensuring that the public workforce is equipped with both foundational and advanced digital skills.

Policy Priority 4: Promoting Innovation and Supporting Entrepreneurship

Promoting Startups through Legal Frameworks and Market Incentives:

To stimulate innovation and entrepreneurship, Libya needs a supportive ecosystem for startups. Drawing inspiration from Tunisia's Startup Act, Libya should develop legal frameworks and investment models that encourage startup growth. This involves creating favourable conditions for venture capital, simplifying business registration processes, and providing tax incentives and other supports to nurture a vibrant startup ecosystem.

Supporting SMEs and Startups:

Building on the OECD's recommendations for SMEs in post-conflict settings, Libya should streamline business registration and licensing processes to reduce bureaucratic hurdles and foster entrepreneurship. Establishing a task force to lead these reforms will help coordinate efforts across government levels and ensure that SMEs and startups receive the support they need to thrive.

Adopting the OECD Going Digital Integrated Policy Framework:

To guide Libya's digital transformation, adopting the OECD Going Digital Toolkit will provide policymakers with the necessary tools to understand digital trends and craft policies that foster a positive digital future. This framework supports the development of integrated policies that encourage digital innovation while ensuring inclusivity and security.

Conclusion and Implementation considerations

A structured, phased approach is essential for transforming Libya's ICT sector into a driver of economic growth and digital inclusion. Implementation should progress through short-, medium-, and long-term objectives, ensuring sustainable development and alignment with global best practices[2].

Short-term priorities include establishing an ICT Business Association to advocate for sector needs and launching training-to-employment programs to bridge the digital skills gap. Strengthening collaboration between the public and private sectors will enhance advocacy efforts and accelerate industry growth.

Medium-term efforts should focus on rolling out basic digital government services to improve transparency and efficiency. These foundational services will support Libya's broader digital governance transition, in line with the General Authority of Communications and Informatics' national strategy. Over the next two to five years, Libya should expand e-government services, strengthen legal frameworks for the digital economy by introducing regulatory frameworks within the relevant institutions, and create a startup-friendly environment inspired by Tunisia's Startup Act. Key reforms should simplify business registration, introduce tax incentives, and foster an innovation-driven ecosystem.

Long-term objectives include the full integration of digital services across public sectors, continuous workforce upskilling in digital competencies, and a flexible ICT policy framework that adapts to technological advancements. Libya's digital governance model should draw from leading examples, such as Estonia, to enhance citizen-government interactions and improve overall efficiency.

The expected economic and social benefits of these reforms are substantial. Digital transformation will diversify Libya's economy, attract foreign investment, and boost productivity. A stronger ICT sector will generate employment, particularly in technology-driven roles, reducing youth unemployment. Additionally, improved digital infrastructure will enhance Libya's competitiveness, elevate citizen satisfaction with public services, and foster civic engagement. By following a structured roadmap and leveraging global lessons, Libya can position ICT as a cornerstone of economic stability and long-term growth, building a resilient, digitally empowered future.

Box 3.3. Tunisia Startup Act – A Regional Model for Enabling Innovation

Adopted in **2018**, Tunisia's **Startup Act** is a pioneering legislative framework designed to foster entrepreneurship and support the growth of innovative startups. It provides a comprehensive set of legal, financial, and institutional incentives to address common challenges faced by startups in the early stages of development.

Key features of the Startup Act include:

- **Startup Label**: An official certification granted by a multidisciplinary committee, allowing eligible startups to access tailored benefits for up to eight years.
- **Tax and Investment Incentives**: Startups enjoy exemptions from corporate taxes, streamlined customs procedures, and access to public and private funding instruments.
- **Support for Founders and Employees**: The Act allows entrepreneurs to take unpaid leave or launch a startup while keeping their jobs and provides stock option frameworks for startup staff.
- **Internationalization and FX Flexibility**: Startups can open foreign currency accounts and conduct transactions with minimal restrictions, supporting cross-border scaling.

Implemented by the **Startup Tunisia initiative** and backed by Smart Capital and the Ministry of ICT, the Act has led to the labelling of hundreds of startups and inspired similar initiatives across Africa and the MENA region. Tunisia's experience offers valuable lessons on how legal reform, ecosystem support, and government buy-in can be combined to create a thriving entrepreneurial environment—even in challenging macroeconomic contexts.

Agriculture

Introduction

Agribusiness is essential for strengthening Libya's resilience to global and regional shocks, improving food security, and supporting sustainable development. Although historically underdeveloped and lacking a clear strategy for reform, the sector holds significant potential for economic diversification and rural revitalisation. Libya remains highly dependent on food imports, covering 75% to 90% of its food needs. In 2020 alone, food imports cost USD 4 billion, consuming a significant share of the national budget (FAO and UNDP, 2021[19]). This dependence, particularly on staple commodities like cereals, makes Libya vulnerable to external shocks such as trade disruptions, price volatility, and global conflicts.

Libya's reliance on wheat imports from Ukraine and Russia illustrates this fragility. Between 2016 and 2020, over 30% of Libya's wheat came from Ukraine and 20% from Russia, exposing the country's food supply to instability following Russia's war of aggression against Ukraine (FAO, 2019[20]). These disruptions have driven up food prices and increased pressure on national food security, underscoring the need for greater domestic agricultural production and resilience-building in agribusiness.

Despite its potential, agriculture contributes only 1.8% to Libya's real GDP, a figure that has remained stagnant due to structural challenges, including outdated farming practices, water scarcity, and limited access to technology (World Bank, 2023[7]). Most production occurs on small farms, with 90% of farms under 20 hectares, making it difficult to meet national demand (WFP, 2020[21]).

Before 2011, 22% of Libyan households engaged in agriculture, with approximately 170,000 farm holders. Of these, 39.4% were full-time farmers, while the rest practiced rainfed, part-time farming (FAO, 2019[20]). However, conflict, economic instability, and rising production costs have forced many farmers to abandon agriculture, contributing to rural displacement and the decline of farming communities (FAO and UNDP, 2021[19]). This exodus has weakened local economies, increased migration to urban centers, and exacerbated Libya's dependence on food imports.

Addressing these challenges requires investment in modernising agriculture, improving irrigation systems, and supporting farmers to rebuild production capacity. Strengthening rural communities will help reduce reliance on imports and mitigate the economic impact of rural displacement.

Context and overview

Libya's agriculture sector remains underdeveloped, contributing just 1.8% to real GDP in 2023, despite engaging 19% of households in agricultural activities. Once a vital part of the economy, the sector has been weakened by decades of underinvestment, political instability, and inefficient farming practices (UNDP, 2021[16]) (Figure 3.9). Its underperformance is a major driver of Libya's heavy reliance on food imports, which supply 75–90% of national food needs, including key staples such as wheat, maize, and barley (FAO, 2021[22]).

Libya remains highly dependent on food imports, particularly cereals, which account for a major share of its import bill. In 2020, over 1.46 million tons of wheat were imported, with 30% from Ukraine and 20% from Russia, exposing the country to supply chain disruptions, especially amid geopolitical instability. These vulnerabilities highlight the urgent need for policies to boost food self-sufficiency and reduce reliance on volatile international markets (World Bank, 2023[7]).

Figure 3.9. Agricultural and related food products remain below its economic potential

Value added, % of GDP

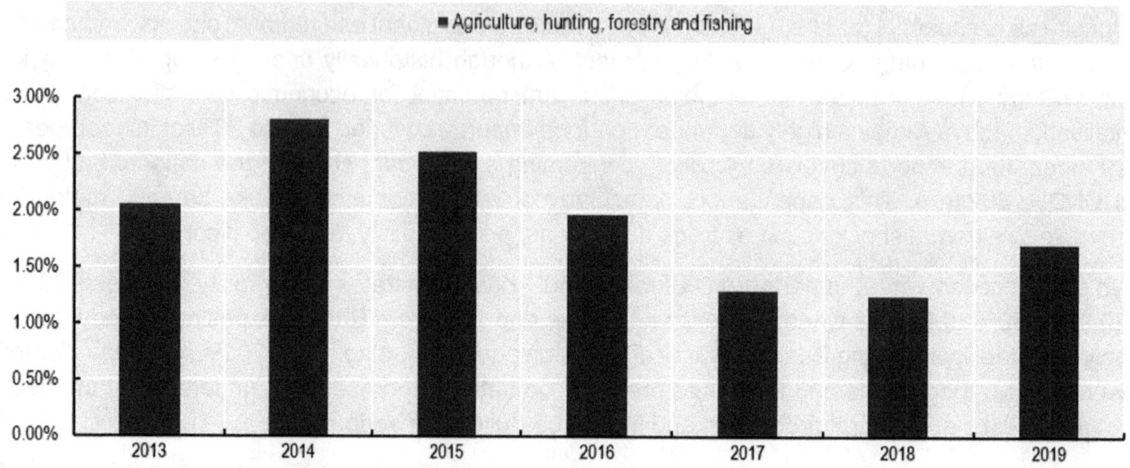

Note: The CBL presents data for fisheries not grouped with agriculture. For simplicity and due to its small size, the OECD has aggregated its value to the later.

Source: OECD Staff calculations, Central Bank of Libya 4th Quarter Economic Bulleting, 2021

Between 2000 and 2013, food production in Libya grew by over 20 percentage points, but this progress stalled due to environmental constraints, limited arable land, and water scarcity, deepening food insecurity. According to the Food Production Index, domestic output has failed to keep pace with demand. In 2020, Libya imported 92% of its cereal needs, underscoring the structural weaknesses in local production (FAO, 2021[22]).

The UNDP projects that a 1% increase in agricultural GDP could generate 35,000 additional jobs with proper investment in infrastructure and modern technologies. Under a favorable investment scenario, the sector could achieve 50% growth in value-added agriculture over three years, supporting employment and economic diversification (UNDP, 2021[16]).

Libya's agricultural sector is dominated by smallholder farms, with 90% of farms under 20 hectares, relying on traditional methods and limited irrigation. While larger agribusinesses exist, they remain underdeveloped, focusing on high-value crops like olives, dates, and select vegetables for export. However, these enterprises face infrastructural deficits and regulatory challenges that hinder expansion (FAO and UNDP, 2021[19]); (World Bank, 2023[7])).

The Ministry of Agriculture, Livestock, and Marine Resources oversees agricultural policy, land management, and regulation, working alongside the Ministry of Water Resources, which manages Libya's scarce water supply. The Agricultural Research Centre (ARC) promotes innovation but struggles with limited funding and resources (FAO and UNDP, 2021[19]).

Governance challenges stem from a fragmented regulatory framework and overlapping institutional roles, leading to inefficiencies and policy inconsistencies. Private sector involvement is constrained by land access difficulties, inconsistent quality standards, and a lack of investment incentives. Reforming governance, improving coordination, and fostering private investment are essential to unlocking agriculture's potential and supporting economic diversification ((World Bank, 2023[7]); (FAO and UNDP, 2021[19])).

Box 3.4. Public-Private Dialogue Process in the Agricultural Sector

The Public-Private Dialogue (PPD) process for Libya's agribusiness sector was undertaken as part of the EU-OECD project to support inclusive reform in key economic sectors. Recognising the sector's potential to enhance food security, create jobs, and promote regional development, the PPD aimed to build consensus on regulatory improvements, strengthen the business environment, and enhance production and export capacities.

The PPD process was rolled out across **three Libyan cities—Benghazi (10–12 October 2022), Sebha (22–24 November 2022), and Misrata (5–7 June 2023)**—adhering to the project's structured three-stage model. Each local engagement included:

1. A **private sector session** to gather insights from entrepreneurs, farmers, and agribusiness companies.
2. A **public sector session** focusing on policy, planning, and regulation.
3. A **joint public-private session**, where shared challenges were validated, and consensus on reform priorities was established.

The three-stage approach allowed each group to speak candidly, identify their most pressing concerns, and build toward mutual understanding. The joint sessions, in particular, were instrumental in showing alignment between public and private stakeholders, and this convergence marked a major success in the PPD's collaborative spirit.

In total, **over 90 participants** from more than **30 institutions** engaged in the dialogues, including the **Ministry of Agriculture, Ministry of Economy and Trade, municipal departments of agriculture, agricultural research institutes, chambers of commerce, private food processing companies, farmers' cooperatives, exporters, and agritech firms**. The sessions were facilitated by the OECD and supported by **Tatweer Research**, which helped coordinate participation across Libya's diverse regions.

The dialogues focused on three core thematic areas:

- **Improving the regulatory framework**: Discussions highlighted outdated laws, bureaucratic overlap, and gaps in quality certification. Participants recommended revising the national agricultural law, introducing incentives for certified production (e.g. organic and GAP certifications), and updating water and land-use policies.
- **Improving the business environment**: Challenges included limited access to finance, weak linkages across the value chain, and insufficient infrastructure. Stakeholders proposed measures such as specialised loan products for agribusinesses, improved cold-chain logistics, and support for innovation hubs to connect smallholders with processors and exporters.
- **Increasing food self-sufficiency and export potential**: Participants identified key opportunities in olive oil, dates, and wheat production, but emphasised the need for modern irrigation methods, stronger market intelligence, and clearer export procedures. Policy roadmaps included awareness campaigns on food safety, simplified customs processes, and targeted support for export-ready agribusinesses.

Concrete proposals emerged from the joint sessions in each city. These included establishing a **national agribusiness development unit**, launching a **"Safe Food Libya" initiative** to improve domestic standards and export readiness, and introducing public-private investment incentives for agro-processing infrastructure.

These proposals were further discussed and refined at the **national PPD meeting in Tunis (29–30 November 2023)**, where the agribusiness reform roadmap was validated by national stakeholders. The roadmap outlines actionable steps to increase sector competitiveness, improve food resilience, and position agribusiness as a pillar of Libya's economic diversification strategy.

Detailed Analysis of Sector Challenges

Libya's agricultural sector faces several interrelated challenges that limit its capacity to contribute to economic diversification, food security, and sustainable development. These challenges arise from supply vulnerabilities, infrastructural deficiencies, economic constraints, and environmental factors.

Supply Vulnerabilities

Libya's heavy reliance on food imports has left the country vulnerable to global market disruptions and geopolitical events, such as Russia's war of aggression to Ukraine. As of 2020, over 30% of Libya's wheat imports came from Ukraine, and an additional 20% from Russia (FAO, 2021[22]). The war in Ukraine has severely impacted the availability and cost of wheat, contributing to food price inflation and exacerbating Libya's food security challenges. The country's reliance on external sources for 75-90% of its food, including essential commodities like wheat, barley, and maize, underscores the urgent need for domestic agricultural development to mitigate risks from global events (World Bank, 2023[7]).

Infrastructural Deficiencies

A lack of critical infrastructure, especially in water management and irrigation, hinders Libya's agricultural growth. The sector consumes 97% of the country's water, drawing primarily from non-renewable groundwater. Over-extraction has lowered water tables and increased salinity, reducing land productivity (FAO, 2021[22]).

Outdated irrigation systems force most farmers to rely on inefficient rainfed agriculture, which limits yields in Libya's arid climate. The country needs modern irrigation technologies like drip and sprinkler systems to conserve water and boost productivity. Additionally, smallholder farmers struggle to access modern machinery, while weak storage, cold chains, and transport networks worsen post-harvest losses, undermining the competitiveness of Libyan agricultural products (FAO and UNDP, 2021[19]).

Economic Challenges

Libya's agriculture sector remains underdeveloped, contributing just 1.8% to real GDP, largely due to the economy's heavy reliance on oil, which dominates government revenues and exports. Minimal investment in non-oil sectors, including agriculture, has hindered growth and diversification (World Bank, 2023[7]).

Volatile oil prices further strain agriculture. When oil prices drop, government revenues shrink, limiting investment in agricultural infrastructure and development programs. The sector also struggles with limited access to credit, weak support for research and innovation, and inadequate extension services. These constraints stifle agricultural growth and prevent it from becoming a stronger driver of economic diversification and job creation (FAO and UNDP, 2021[19]).

Environmental and Climatic Challenges

Libya's arid climate and scarcity of natural water resources are key environmental challenges for the agricultural sector. The country experiences limited rainfall, high rates of evapotranspiration, and lacks surface water bodies. As a result, most of Libya's agricultural activities are dependent on non-renewable groundwater, which is rapidly being depleted due to over-extraction (FAO, 2021[22]).

To address these issues, Libya must adopt more sustainable agricultural practices. Solar-powered irrigation systems (SPIS) present a viable solution for regulating water use and providing energy access to rural areas. Libya has one of the highest solar radiation levels in the world, with an average of 7.1 kWh/m²/day. Leveraging this solar potential for agriculture could mitigate water scarcity and reduce the sector's reliance on non-renewable energy sources (FAO, 2021[22]). However, the widespread adoption of such systems requires a transparent and supportive regulatory framework that encourages private sector investment and integrates solar energy strategies into national water management plans.

Strategic Priorities and Policy Recommendations

To overcome the significant challenges facing the agriculture sector, Libya must pursue a series of targeted reforms and investments aimed at enhancing productivity, sustainability, and market integration. These recommendations are rooted in OECD best practices but tailored to the unique circumstances of Libya's agricultural landscape.

Policy Priority 1: Improving the Regulatory Framework

I. Reinforce Integration with International Markets

Libya's weak regulatory framework has hindered its integration into international agricultural markets. The absence of regulations for quality control, certification, and grading standards results in lower productivity and limits the sector's export potential. To address this, Libya needs to adopt internationally recognised standards for agricultural inputs, production processes, and product certification. Implementing Good Agricultural Practices (GAP) and organic certifications would allow Libya to tap into premium export markets, particularly for high-value products such as dates and olive oil (FAO and UNDP, 2021[19]).

In addition to quality control, food safety measures, and packaging standards, Libya must invest in traceability systems to enhance its competitiveness in global markets. Strengthening market-oriented policies that focus on promoting export diversification and building international partnerships would also improve Libya's participation in the global agri-food market (OECD, 2016[3]).

II. Modernise Agricultural Input Markets.

High input costs and reliance on the black market for seeds, fertilisers, and pesticides have stunted Libya's agricultural growth. OECD best practices recommend creating transparent input markets, where the government can regulate and monitor the quality and pricing of agricultural inputs. This can be achieved by setting up quality control mechanisms and improving distribution channels, particularly in rural areas. Introducing subsidies for certified, high-quality inputs could incentivise farmers to move away from low-cost, low-quality alternatives (FAO and UNDP, 2021[19]).

Policy Priority 2: Improving the Business Environment

I. Support Research, Innovation, and Technology Transfer

A key barrier to the growth of Libya's agriculture sector is the lack of investment in research, innovation, and technology transfer. The government should prioritise expanding agricultural research centres and extension services to enhance knowledge sharing and technical support. In line with OECD best practices, Libya must foster partnerships between the public sector, academia, and international research institutions to stimulate innovation and promote the adoption of climate-smart agricultural technologies (OECD, 2020[14]).

A focus on technology transfer, particularly in post-harvest handling and value-added processing, would improve Libya's agricultural productivity. Integrating digital solutions, such as precision farming and mobile advisory services, can help smallholder farmers increase yields and reduce inefficiencies (FAO and UNDP, 2021[19]). Capacity-building programs for farmers, focused on modern agronomic techniques and water management, are essential to ensure sustainable productivity growth.

II. Foster Sustainable Productivity Growth

Water scarcity remains one of the most pressing challenges for Libya's agriculture. Given the country's reliance on non-renewable groundwater, immediate steps must be taken to manage water resources more sustainably. Investments in modern irrigation systems, such as drip and sprinkler technologies, are essential to reduce water wastage and increase efficiency (FAO, 2021[22]). Libya must also develop policies that incentivise water conservation and promote the use of treated wastewater in agriculture.

Solar-powered irrigation systems (SPIS) offer a sustainable solution to Libya's energy and water challenges. By leveraging the country's high solar radiation levels, SPIS can reduce reliance on fossil fuels and enhance access to energy in rural areas. However, the success of this initiative depends on creating a clear regulatory framework that encourages private sector investment and integrates SPIS into national water management strategies (FAO, 2021[22]).

Policy Priority 3: Increasing Libya's Food Self-Sufficiency and Export Potential

I. Optimise Agribusiness Production and Export Capacity

Libya holds significant potential for producing high-value crops such as olives, dates, and vegetables, particularly for export markets. To capitalise on this, Libya must improve its agricultural supply chains and logistics infrastructure, especially in transportation, storage, and cold chain management. Addressing these bottlenecks will reduce post-harvest losses and enable the country to meet international quality standards (FAO and UNDP, 2021[19]).

Libya can build on the OECD good policy practices in making its agri-business development more market-driven, focusing on strengthening the linkages between farmers and export markets. By improving access to market information, enhancing quality control, and facilitating trade logistics, Libya can boost its competitiveness in the global market. Investments in rural infrastructure, such as roads and storage facilities, are also critical for improving market access for smallholder farmers and fostering economic growth in rural areas (OECD, 2020[3]).

II. Promote Sustainable Agricultural Practices and Climate Adaptation.

Given the environmental challenges posed by Libya's arid climate, promoting sustainable agricultural practices is essential for long-term productivity. OECD best practices emphasise the importance of integrating climate resilience into national agricultural policies. Libya should focus on promoting organic farming, agroforestry, and conservation agriculture, which improve soil health, reduce water usage, and mitigate the impacts of climate change (FAO and UNDP, 2021[19]).

Educating farmers on the benefits of organic farming and sustainable land management practices will not only enhance productivity but also position Libyan agricultural products favourably in international markets. In addition, adopting renewable energy sources such as solar power for agricultural operations aligns with global environmental goals and contributes to energy self-sufficiency (FAO, 2021[22]).

Conclusion

Revitalising Libya's agricultural sector is essential for economic diversification, food security, and resilience to external shocks. Despite challenges such as regulatory gaps, weak infrastructure, and environmental constraints, strategic reforms and targeted investments could transform agribusiness into a competitive, high-performing sector that strengthens national food security and economic growth.

Short-Term Priorities. Libya must establish a robust regulatory framework focused on quality control, certification, and market integration. Implementing Good Agricultural Practices (GAP) and organic certification for high-value crops like dates and olives would help Libya tap into lucrative international markets. Reforming agricultural input markets to ensure access to high-quality seeds, fertilisers, and pesticides through regulated supply chains is critical to reducing reliance on the black market, where poor-quality inputs hinder productivity. Public awareness campaigns can educate farmers on sustainable practices, including water conservation and climate-smart agriculture.

Medium-Term Investments. Modernising irrigation systems, rural transportation, and cold storage will improve productivity and reduce post-harvest losses. Public-private partnerships (PPPs) can drive technology and knowledge transfer in post-harvest handling, value-added processing, and modern farming techniques. Integrating solar-powered irrigation systems (SPIS) into the national water management strategy would provide energy-efficient solutions to water scarcity.

Long-Term Development. Sustained rural investment should encourage youth and women to participate in agriculture, ensuring workforce expansion and long-term sustainability. Strengthening trade linkages with global markets will integrate Libya's agribusiness into international supply chains. National research and innovation hubs will drive continuous productivity and sustainability improvements, keeping Libya competitive in international markets.

By addressing regulatory and infrastructure deficiencies, Libya can boost agricultural productivity and reduce food import dependency, which currently covers up to 90% of national consumption. Strengthening domestic production will also generate employment, particularly in rural areas. Every 1% increase in agricultural GDP could create 35,000 new jobs, contributing to broader economic stability (UNDP, 2021[16]).

Expanding access to international markets, improving connectivity to sustainable value chains and improving export quality could generate significant foreign exchange earnings from crops like olives, dates, and vegetables, reducing dependence on volatile oil revenues. Adopting sustainable practices, including SPIS and organic farming, will mitigate water scarcity and soil degradation, ensuring long-term agricultural resilience.

MENA countries offer valuable models for Libya's agricultural transformation. Morocco's Green Morocco Plan has successfully promoted sustainable resource management, value-added processing, and export market integration. Its use of solar-powered irrigation has improved water efficiency in arid regions, providing a viable model for Libya (FAO, 2021[22]). Tunisia's focus on organic farming and quality certification programs has secured access to premium European markets, offering a blueprint for Libya to enhance its export competitiveness (OECD, 2016[15]).

Despite its challenges, Libya's agricultural sector holds immense potential. Strengthening regulatory frameworks, infrastructure, and sustainable practices can unlock agribusiness growth, ensuring food security, economic diversification, and long-term resilience. Achieving this transformation requires coordinated efforts across government, private sector, and international partners, but with the right reforms, Libya can build a sustainable and prosperous future.

Infrastructure

Infrastructure serves as the backbone of economic growth, enhancing productivity, innovation, and competitiveness. High-quality infrastructure reduces logistics costs, improves market access, and strengthens participation in global value chains. It also expands access to essential services like education, healthcare, and sanitation, improving quality of life and economic opportunities for both businesses and citizens (OECD, 2021[23]). Years of conflict have severely weakened Libya's infrastructure, making its rehabilitation and modernisation essential for economic recovery and long-term stability.

Infrastructure encompasses two key dimensions: social and economic; both are essential for Libya's development. Social infrastructure, including healthcare, education, water supply, and public housing, enhances well-being and human capital. Economic infrastructure, such as transportation networks, energy systems, telecommunications, and industrial facilities, drives productivity and economic expansion. Strengthening both is crucial to rebuilding Libya's economy and addressing regional disparities, particularly in the east and south, which remain disadvantaged (World Bank, 2023[7]).

Decades of underinvestment and conflict have left key sectors such as electricity, water, sanitation, and transport outdated or non-functional, hindering economic activity and public welfare. The 2023 floods further exposed infrastructure vulnerabilities, particularly in water and power supply systems (World Bank, 2023[7]). However, reconstruction presents an opportunity to build a more resilient, diversified economy by prioritising modern infrastructure investments that support sustainable development.

A well-planned infrastructure strategy can enhance governance, improve planning transparency, and strengthen regulatory frameworks to ensure cost-efficient and sustainable projects (OECD, 2017[24]). Investments in roads, electricity grids, water management, and modernised ports and airports will help create a more connected and economically dynamic Libya. Additionally, upgrading infrastructure will facilitate growth in emerging sectors, such as renewable energy and ICT, reducing Libya's dependence on oil revenues (OECD, 2021[25]).

Given funding constraints, public-private partnerships (PPPs) will be essential for financing and executing large-scale infrastructure projects (OECD, 2007[26]). International organisations, including the OECD and World Bank, can provide guidance and best practices, such as the OECD Principles for Private Sector Participation in Infrastructure, to help Libya attract investment and improve infrastructure governance (OECD, 2007[26]).

Box 3.5. International Standards and Initiatives for Quality Infrastructure Development

In the pursuit of rebuilding and modernising its infrastructure, Libya can benefit from aligning with established international frameworks and initiatives that promote quality, sustainability, and resilience in infrastructure projects.

OECD Recommendation on the Governance of Infrastructure

The OECD has developed comprehensive guidelines to assist governments in ensuring that infrastructure projects are cost-effective, affordable, and trusted by stakeholders. These recommendations emphasise strategic planning, transparent decision-making, and robust regulatory frameworks to enhance the governance of infrastructure investments.

EU Global Gateway Initiative

Launched in 2021, the European Union's Global Gateway is a strategy aimed at boosting smart, clean, and secure links in digital, energy, and transport sectors, while strengthening health, education, and research systems globally. With a commitment to mobilise up to €300 billion in investments by 2027, the initiative focuses on democratic values, good governance, and equal partnerships, offering a framework for sustainable infrastructure development that Libya could leverage.

Blue Dot Network

The Blue Dot Network is a multilateral initiative that provides a certification framework for quality infrastructure projects, ensuring they adhere to high standards of transparency, sustainability, and developmental impact. Supported by countries including Australia, Japan, and the United States, this network aims to promote trusted standards and attract private sector investment into certified projects.

By engaging with these international standards and initiatives, Libya can enhance the quality and sustainability of its infrastructure projects, attract foreign investment, and ensure that development efforts are inclusive and resilient.

Economic Context and Current State of the Infrastructure Sector in Libya

Libya's infrastructure sector operates within a fragmented governance framework, shaped by political instability and weak institutional coordination. State-owned enterprises (SOEs) dominate the sector, managing key utilities like electricity, water, and transportation. The General Electricity Company of Libya (GECOL) and the General Company for Water and Wastewater oversee electricity and water services, respectively. However, these SOEs struggle with inefficiencies, underfunding, and limited capacity to handle large-scale projects, resulting in frequent service disruptions and slow infrastructure development.

The private sector's role in infrastructure remains limited but is gradually expanding, mainly through small and medium-sized enterprises (SMEs) engaged in construction, maintenance, and service delivery. Private sector participation is hindered by regulatory barriers, including restrictive investment laws and complex procurement processes that reduce competition and transparency. The establishment of the Libyan Public-Private Partnership (PPP) Company in 2020 aimed to increase private sector engagement, yet the lack of a comprehensive PPP framework has slowed progress.

Government oversight remains fragmented, with responsibilities divided across multiple ministries and agencies. The Ministry of Planning and the Ministry of Housing and Utilities play central roles in project approval and resource allocation, but the absence of a cohesive national infrastructure strategy and weak inter-agency coordination lead to inefficiencies and delays. Strengthening governance frameworks, improving procurement transparency, and reforming SOEs will be essential to boosting infrastructure performance and attracting investment for Libya's reconstruction and long-term development.

Despite political instability and conflict, Libya's infrastructure sector has shown resilience. Unlike other non-oil economic activities, construction and infrastructure-related sectors have experienced a milder downturn. Data from the Central Bank of Libya (CBL) indicates that in 2019, infrastructure-related activities contributed 1.76% to GDP, slightly up from 1.7% in 2013 (Figure 3.10). In gross economic volume, the sector expanded to LYD 1.9 billion in 2019, compared to LYD 1.7 billion in 2013 (respectively USD 1.54 billion and 1.36 billion, at 2013 values). Although the sector hit a low point in 2017, dropping 23% below the current maximum, it has since rebounded, highlighting its capacity to withstand economic shocks (CBL, 2021[10]).

Figure 3.10. Construction is among the most resilient economic sectors in Libya

Value added, % of GDP - 2019

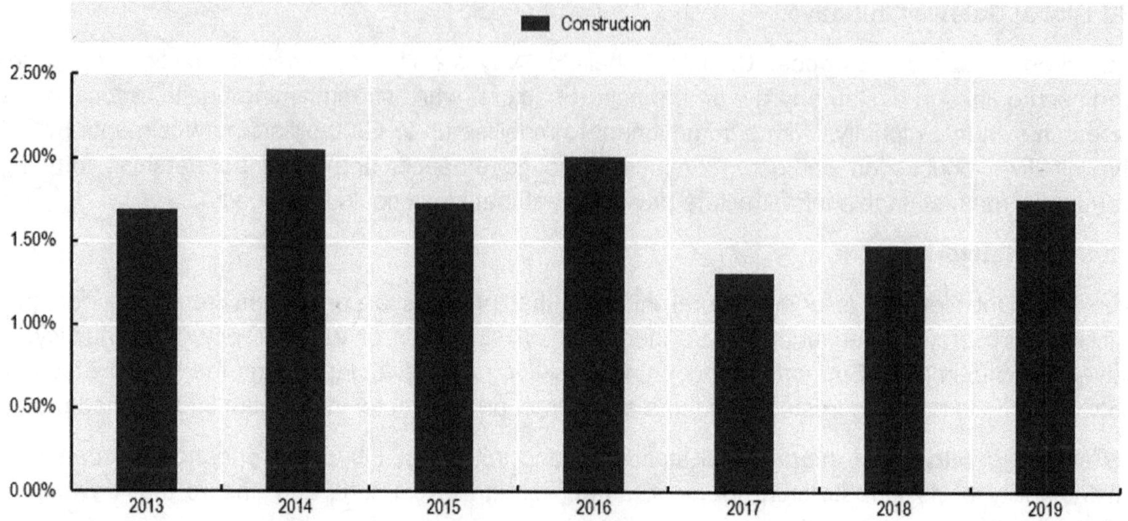

Source: OECD Staff calculations, Central Bank of Libya 4th Quarter Economic Bulletin, 2021

Despite recent improvements, Libya's infrastructure sector faces significant challenges. Conflict has severely damaged water, sanitation, electricity, and transportation systems, further exacerbated by the 2023 floods. As noted in the World Bank's 2023 Libya Economic Monitor, this destruction has constrained the government's ability to deliver essential services, with damaged roads, unreliable power, and inadequate water supply hindering economic recovery (World Bank, 2023[7]).

The construction sector, closely tied to infrastructure, is a key driver of job creation, employing around 2% of Libya's workforce in 2020-2021 (Juillard et al., 2021[27]). Migrant labor accounts for 37% of the sector, filling critical skill gaps. The UNDP highlights construction as a high-potential sector for economic growth, projecting a 35% increase in activity and a 26% rise in employment (UNDP, 2021[16]). With targeted support, the sector could generate over 70,000 jobs in the short-to-medium term, contributing 1% to GDP (Juillard et al., 2021[27]).

Libya has also expanded production and exports of construction materials such as iron, steel, copper, and cement, signalling opportunities for industrial policy to strengthen both infrastructure and manufacturing. The OECD has identified infrastructure as a priority for FDI and industrial development, emphasising its role in economic diversification and job creation (OECD, 2016[3]).

Box 3.6. Public-Private Dialogue Process in the Infrastructure Sector

The infrastructure sector was a central focus of the EU-OECD Project on Promoting Public-Private Dialogue (PPD) in Libya, recognising its critical role in enabling economic recovery and long-term development. The PPD sessions provided a structured platform for stakeholders to engage on financing, regulatory, and governance challenges facing the sector, and to propose practical, locally grounded solutions to revive investment and improve service delivery.

PPD sessions for infrastructure were held in **Benghazi (12–15 September 2022), Sebha (29 November–1 December 2022), and Tripoli (22–24 May 2023)**. Each round followed the project's **three-stage format**, beginning with separate dialogues with private and public sector stakeholders to identify sector-specific challenges. The process culminated in a joint session where both groups validated the findings and co-developed reform initiatives. This sequencing allowed for the safe articulation of concerns and ultimately highlighted convergence on core priorities—an early indication of the dialogue's success in building trust.

More than **60 participants** representing over **30 public and private institutions** took part across the three cities. Participants included representatives from the **Ministry of Planning, General Authority for Communications and Infrastructure, General Authority for Roads and Bridges, General Electricity Company of Libya (GECOL), the Public-Private Partnership Company**, as well as local construction firms, engineering consultancies, infrastructure financing experts, and regional chambers of commerce.

Three main thematic areas were tackled in these dialogues:

- **Improving Financing of Infrastructure**: Participants raised concerns over the lack of private investment due to legal uncertainty, high risk, and the absence of effective guarantees. Solutions included the establishment of risk-sharing mechanisms, reform of procurement laws, and the need to activate the long-pending Public-Private Partnership (PPP) Law to encourage private sector involvement.
- **Improving Regulatory Framework and Governance of Infrastructure Delivery**: Discussion focused on the inefficiency of state-owned enterprises (SOEs), weak coordination among agencies, and lack of accountability in project delivery. Recommendations included restructuring SOEs, outsourcing non-core functions to the private sector, and introducing new performance benchmarks and procurement standards.
- **Expanding Public-Private Partnerships (PPPs)**: Participants acknowledged that PPPs offer essential avenues for funding and managing infrastructure. The joint sessions called for the creation of specialised PPP units within ministries and the introduction of a transparent framework to govern project selection, contractor engagement, and performance monitoring.

A number of actionable initiatives emerged from the joint sessions. These included the **activation of a national infrastructure investment framework**, the creation of **regional project pipelines**, and a **PPP capacity-building programme** for line ministries and municipal authorities. The proposals were consolidated into a reform roadmap and validated during the **national PPD session in Tunis (29–30 November 2023)**, setting the foundation for coordinated implementation.

The infrastructure PPDs demonstrated how structured dialogue, even in fragile contexts, can bridge institutional divides and promote shared ownership of national development priorities.

Challenges Facing the Infrastructure Sector in Libya

Libya's infrastructure sector struggles with conflict, political instability, and weak governance. Challenges stem from inadequate policies, underinvestment in non-oil sectors, and capacity constraints. Strengthening these areas is crucial for improving efficiency and supporting economic recovery.

Governance and Regulatory Issues

One of the most significant barriers to infrastructure development in Libya is the lack of coherent governance and regulatory frameworks. The country's infrastructure policy is fragmented, with overlapping jurisdictions and inconsistent regulatory enforcement across sectors. This fragmented governance structure has resulted in the inefficient allocation of resources and slow decision-making processes, particularly in critical sectors such as water, sanitation, and transportation (World Bank, 2023[7]).

Moreover, Libya's regulatory environment for infrastructure investment lacks transparency, which discourages private sector involvement, particularly foreign direct investment (FDI) (Figure 3.11). In the absence of clear policies, private investors face uncertainty regarding the return on investment and the legal protections available to them. As a result, the country has struggled to attract significant FDI, particularly in sectors outside of oil and gas, which remain the primary focus of government policies (OECD, 2017[24]). The weak governance framework also hinders the development of public-private partnerships (PPPs), a key mechanism for mobilising private capital and expertise in infrastructure development (OECD, 2007[26]).

Figure 3.11. OECD FDI Regulatory Restrictiveness Index in selected sectors

Closed=1; Open=0 (2020)

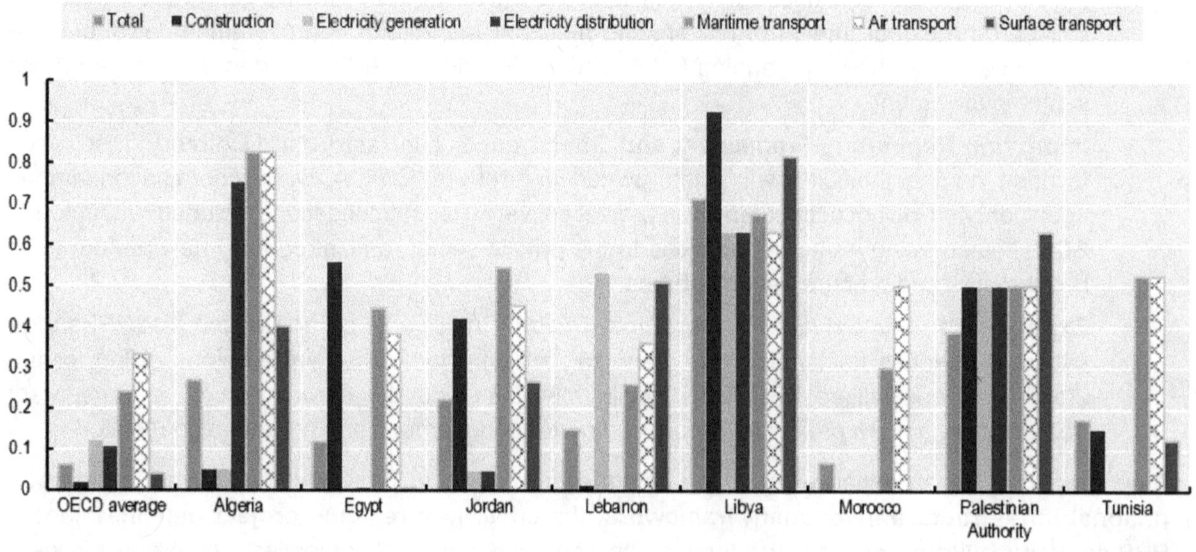

Source: OECD, 2020

Public Investment Deficiencies

Libya's dependence on oil revenues has skewed public investment, with over 70% of capital expenditure historically allocated to the National Oil Corporation (NOC) and security, leaving critical infrastructure underfunded (World Bank, 2023[7]). Water, sanitation, and transportation have suffered as a result, with the 2023 floods exposing the fragility of water infrastructure and worsening public health risks (World Bank, 2023[7]). Poor road networks and inadequate public transport further deepen regional disparities, particularly between urban centers in the west and underdeveloped areas in the east and south (OECD, 2017[24]). This neglect hinders economic diversification and limits infrastructure's role in sustainable growth and development.

Capacity Constraints

Libya's infrastructure sector faces severe capacity constraints in project management, technical expertise, and workforce skills. Decades of conflict have depleted skilled professionals, particularly in engineering and construction, while brain drain has worsened the shortage (Juillard et al., 2021[27]).

The lack of expertise delays projects, inflates costs, and weakens public confidence, deterring private investment. Migrant workers fill many construction jobs, but higher-skilled positions remain vacant, limiting infrastructure development (Juillard et al., 2021[27]). Institutional weaknesses further hinder progress, as ministries and agencies struggle with inadequate technical expertise and resources, leading to fragmented, unsustainable infrastructure planning (World Bank, 2023[7]).

Strategic Priorities and Policy Recommendations

To address the significant challenges facing Libya's infrastructure sector, targeted reforms and strategic investments are essential to improve governance, attract investment, and enhance service delivery. These recommendations are grounded in OECD best practices but are tailored to Libya's unique post-conflict context.

Policy Priority 1: Improve Financing of Infrastructure

I. Attract Foreign Direct Investment (FDI) for Reconstruction

Attracting FDI is essential for Libya's reconstruction, offering financial resources, knowledge transfer, job creation, and innovation. However, regulatory barriers—such as equity limits, discriminatory screening, and land ownership restrictions—continue to hinder foreign investment (OECD, 2022[28]).

Despite reforms, including those in 2010, challenges persist, particularly in infrastructure, where foreign investors must often form joint ventures, limiting full ownership and control (OECD, 2016[15]). Removing these barriers is key to securing high-quality FDI that can drive infrastructure development.

To attract international investment in infrastructure, Libya should revise investment laws to ease ownership restrictions in key sectors such as water, sanitation, and energy. Establishing transparent investment guidelines will provide clarity on market entry and project management, enhancing investor confidence. Additionally, introducing incentive structures such as tax breaks and guarantees can further encourage foreign participation. Clear legislation defining the state's role in project selection and contractor engagement is also essential to ensure transparency and foster international collaboration.

Policy Priority 2: Improve Governance of Infrastructure Delivery

I. Facilitate Better Service Delivery

Libya's state-controlled electricity and water sectors have long been plagued by inefficiencies. Frequent power outages and water shortages have disrupted businesses and communities alike, with many companies forced to invest in costly generators. The 2023 floods highlighted the vulnerabilities of Libya's water infrastructure (World Bank, 2023[7]).

To improve service delivery, it is essential to strengthen competition in the infrastructure sector. State-owned enterprises (SOEs) dominate service provision, limiting private sector involvement. Small and medium enterprises (SMEs) also face difficulties competing for public tenders due to high entry costs and complex procurement processes (OECD, 2016[3]). Reforming procurement laws and improving the regulatory framework can help increase competition, boost efficiency, and enhance service quality.

To enhance infrastructure development, Libya should reform public procurement laws to promote fair competition, particularly for SMEs, by reducing bidding costs and increasing transparency. Encouraging private sector participation in service delivery, especially in underperforming areas such as electricity and water, will help improve efficiency. Strengthening regulatory frameworks is also essential to ensure infrastructure services meet international standards. Additionally, enforcing procurement regulations that prioritise transparency and fair competition—making public tenders the standard practice—will foster a more open and accountable investment environment.

II. Reform State-Owned Enterprises (SOEs)

Libya's infrastructure-related SOEs are inefficient, overstaffed, and lack the technical capacity for large-scale projects. Reform is crucial to improve service delivery and reduce costs (OECD, 2021[23]). Outsourcing functions like project management and maintenance to the private sector could enhance efficiency, while restructuring should prioritise financial sustainability and operational performance.

To improve infrastructure financing, the Libyan government should take several key actions. Revising investment laws to ease ownership restrictions in critical sectors such as water, sanitation, and energy would attract more private investment. Establishing transparent investment guidelines would provide foreign companies with clear market entry and project management frameworks, enhancing investor confidence. Additionally, introducing incentives such as tax breaks and guarantees could further encourage international investment in infrastructure projects. Finally, developing legislation that clearly defines the state's role in project selection and contractor engagement would ensure transparency and foster greater international collaboration.

Policy Priority 3: Increase Public-Private Partnerships (PPPs) in Infrastructure

I. Increase Public-Private Partnerships

Expanding public-private partnerships (PPPs) can help address Libya's infrastructure needs by leveraging private investment and expertise. However, the country lacks a robust PPP framework, with a draft law still pending legislative approval (Rahman and Di Maio, 2020[9]). Establishing a clear legal framework with risk-sharing mechanisms would enhance investor confidence, encourage private sector participation, and strengthen public-private collaboration.

To strengthen public-private partnerships (PPPs) in infrastructure development, the Libyan government should enact the draft PPP law to establish a clear legal framework for private sector participation. Creating specialised PPP units within government agencies would improve project oversight, coordination, and accountability. Additionally, developing risk-sharing mechanisms would protect both public and private stakeholders, making infrastructure investments more attractive. Ensuring transparency and mutual benefits in PPP arrangements would further build trust between the public and private sectors, encouraging greater private sector engagement in infrastructure projects.

Conclusion and implementation considerations

Rebuilding and modernising Libya's infrastructure is essential for economic recovery and long-term development. This paper outlines strategic priorities and policy recommendations focusing on three key areas: improving financing, enhancing governance, and increasing private sector involvement. Implementing these reforms will unlock the infrastructure sector's potential, fostering economic stability and growth.

Short term: Addressing financing challenges is the first step, primarily through attracting foreign direct investment (FDI). Revising investment laws to ease ownership restrictions and establishing transparent guidelines will help mobilise capital for infrastructure reconstruction. Clear legislation on project selection and contractor engagement, along with incentives like tax breaks, can further enhance Libya's investment appeal. A robust legal framework for public-private partnerships (PPPs) will also be critical in securing private sector participation, bringing both financial resources and technical expertise.

Medium term: Streamlining procurement regulations to promote fair competition and transparency, particularly for small and medium-sized enterprises (SMEs), will strengthen trust and improve service delivery in electricity and water sectors. State-owned enterprises (SOEs) must be restructured to enhance efficiency and financial sustainability. Outsourcing non-core functions, setting performance benchmarks, and creating oversight mechanisms for stalled projects will help redirect government focus to larger strategic infrastructure investments.

Long term: Strengthening financing and governance will significantly improve essential services such as electricity, water, transportation, and telecommunications. This will enhance citizens' quality of life, lower business costs, and create a more stable environment for economic growth. Expanding PPPs will alleviate fiscal pressures while fostering innovation and knowledge transfer, further supporting Libya's development.

Case studies from post-conflict economies highlight the transformative impact of infrastructure reform. In Rwanda, PPPs and FDI-driven post-genocide reconstruction led to rapid improvements in energy and transport networks, while regulatory reforms encouraged foreign investment. Iraq's post-war reconstruction focused on governance and procurement transparency, attracting investment and improving public services. Libya can draw key lessons from these experiences, particularly in governance, financing, and private sector engagement.

Conclusion: The recommendations outlined in this paper provide a clear roadmap for revitalising Libya's infrastructure sector. Implementing these reforms will not only rebuild physical infrastructure but also drive economic diversification, job creation, and social stability. By aligning its strategies with international best practices, Libya can transform its infrastructure sector into a pillar of sustainable development, benefiting both its citizens and economy for years to come.

Transportation

The transportation sector in Libya is critically linked to the country's economic vitality yet remains one of the most substantial obstacles to its growth. The sector's challenges are exacerbated by ongoing conflict, which has caused severe damage to infrastructure and significantly disrupted logistics operations. According to the World Bank, over half of the firms surveyed identify transportation as a major constraint to business operations, a sentiment particularly acute in Libya's Southern region where disruptions surpass the national average by a significant margin due to frequent clashes that damage roads and hinder transit (World Bank, 2023[7]).

This backdrop of conflict has escalated transportation constraints dramatically since 2013, with nearly half of all firms nationally—and virtually all firms in the Southern region—reporting worsening conditions. The degradation of state institutions and the resultant vacuum of authority have allowed non-state armed groups to exploit the transportation network for financial gain through various illicit activities. Predation on the transport of goods, extortion at both official and makeshift checkpoints, and forced security payments have become commonplace, imposing additional costs on businesses, and stifling economic activities (World Bank, 2023[7]).

These non-state actors leverage the lack of security to extort businesses, significantly inflating transportation, and security expenses. Such increased costs not only raise the price of inputs but also push businesses to consider relocating or ceasing operations altogether. Specifically, firms in trade and construction are disproportionately affected, facing heightened burdens of additional, often illicit, costs related to transportation, particularly in the strife-ridden Southern region. This scenario underscores a critical need for a strategic overhaul of the transportation sector, aimed at reinforcing infrastructure, enhancing regulatory frameworks, and restoring state control to revitalise Libya's economic landscape.

Context and Overview

Libya's transportation sector operates within a fragile context, shaped by state institutions and private enterprises. It includes road, maritime, and air transport, with roads being the most widely used but severely degraded due to conflict and underinvestment.

Libya's transport infrastructure consists of a basic but underutilised and deteriorating network of facilities. The country has **10 commercial airports**, though only a few—such as Mitiga, Benina, and Misrata—are currently operating at partial capacity due to conflict-related damage and limited investment (World Bank, 2023[7]). Its **major seaports**, including Tripoli, Misrata, Benghazi, and Tobruk, serve as key gateways for imports, but suffer from ageing infrastructure and limited connectivity to inland distribution networks. Libya also possesses an estimated 3,000 km of railway tracks, though none are currently operational. Most railway infrastructure was either abandoned or left incomplete due to political instability and stalled foreign partnerships, particularly with China and Russia ((OECD, 2020[29]); (World Bank, 2023[7])). The lack of integration between ports, airports, and road infrastructure further compounds the inefficiency of the current transport system and limits its potential as an engine for economic diversification and regional connectivity.

The private sector plays a growing role, particularly in logistics, freight forwarding, and port operations. The Misrata Free Zone has emerged as a key hub, attracting businesses in shipping, warehousing, and manufacturing. However, inadequate infrastructure, high costs, and an unclear regulatory framework hinder private sector expansion. SMEs dominate the sector but struggle with financing and bureaucratic barriers, while informal actors further complicate competition.

Governance is fragmented, with multiple institutions overseeing different aspects of transport. The Ministry of Transportation handles policy, the General Authority for Roads and Bridges manages road infrastructure, and separate agencies regulate aviation and maritime transport. Overlapping responsibilities lead to inefficiencies, though international organisations like the World Bank and the EU have supported efforts to improve coordination and infrastructure investment (World Bank, 2023[7]).

Despite some governance improvements, significant reform is needed to attract investment and integrate Libya into global trade networks. The Central Bank of Libya's first sectoral data report since 2014 highlights a sharp decline in gross value added, from LYD 6.3 billion in 2013 to LYD 2.1 billion in 2019 (respectively USD 4.98 billion, and USD 432 million), reflecting the broader economic downturn driven by conflict and infrastructure decline ((CBL, 2021[10]); (OECD, 2016[15])) (Figure 3.12).

Figure 3.12. Libya's evolution of transport, storage and telecommunications services value added since 2013

Value added, % of GDP

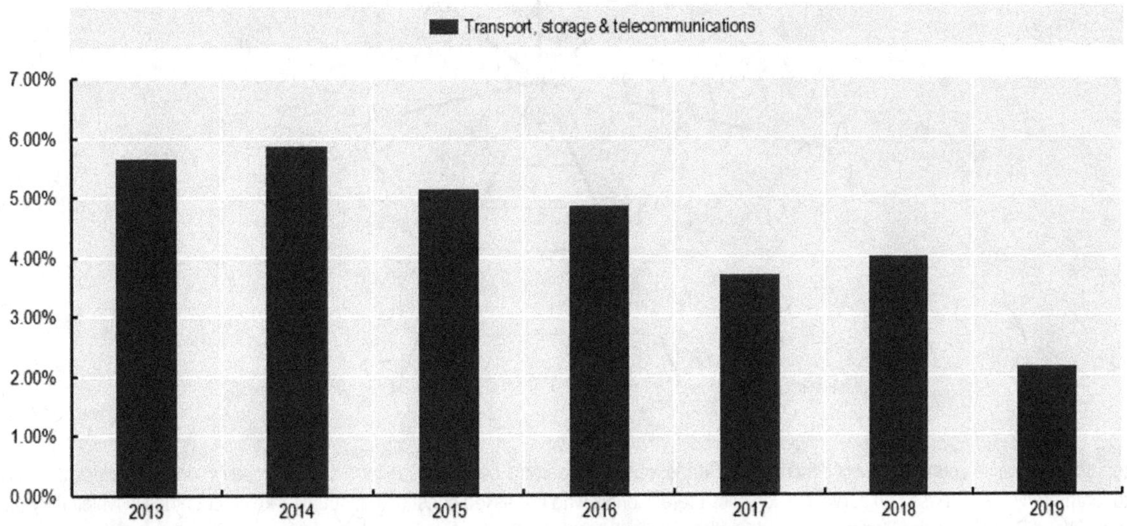

Source: OECD Staff calculations, Central Bank of Libya 4th Quarter Economic Bulleting, 2021

Trade data from the IMF's Direction of Trade Statistics (DOTS) highlights structural weaknesses in Libya's transportation sector. By 2019, transport service exports had fallen to 49% of their 2013 levels, while imports were 20 times higher than exports—double the mid-to-late 2000s average—underscoring heavy reliance on foreign services. The degradation of the transport infrastructure is reflected by Libya low performance in terms of logistics, regionally (Figure 3.13).

OECD stakeholder consultations emphasised the sector's potential for job creation and economic diversification. Similarly, the World Bank's 2020 survey identified transport and logistics as key drivers of growth due to Libya's dependence on imported goods. The survey recommended tackling constraints such as access to finance, unreliable electricity, deteriorating roads, and a shortage of skilled labour to support sector recovery and expansion (World Bank, 2021[1]).

Figure 3.13. Libya scores low in the Logistics Performance Index in the MENA region, 2018

Score from 0 to 5 (best)

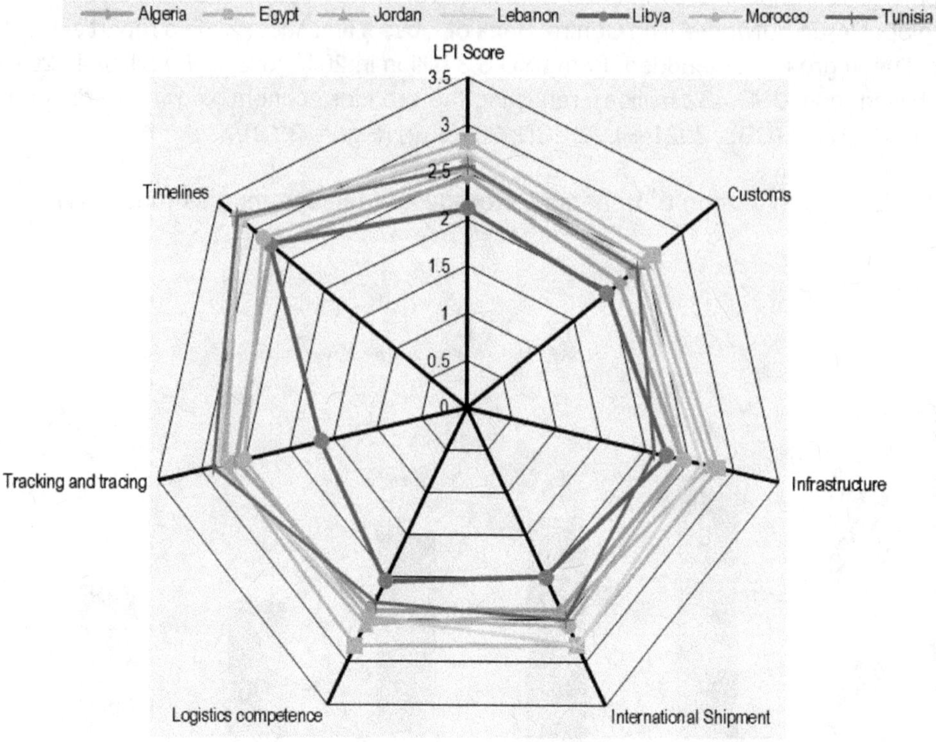

Note: LPI 2018 ranks countries on six dimensions of trade, covering customs performance, infrastructure quality, and timeliness of shipments. Data for the ranking are based on surveys of logistics professionals who are asked questions about the foreign countries in which they operate.
Source: World Bank, Logistics Performance Index, https://lpi.worldbank.org/

The transportation sector, despite being heavily characterised by informal employment, remains crucial for Libya's economic stability and supply chain resilience. Reports from UNDP (2021) and IOM (2021) indicate that while its direct economic output is limited, its strategic role in connecting Libya's vast territory is vital for economic integration. Data and stakeholder consultations highlight both challenges and potential. With strategic investments and targeted policy reforms, the sector could become a key pillar of Libya's economic recovery and development (UNDP, 2021[16]).

Box 3.7. Public-Private Dialogue Process in the Transport Sector

The Public-Private Dialogue (PPD) process for Libya's transportation sector was a core component of the EU-OECD project's mission to address critical barriers to mobility, trade, and logistics. Recognizing the sector's essential role in economic recovery and regional integration, the PPD sought to create a space where both public institutions and private actors could jointly define challenges and develop actionable solutions.

The transport dialogues took place in **Benghazi (4–6 October 2022), Sebha (8–10 December 2022), and Misrata (12–14 June 2023)**, following the structured **three-stage dialogue format**. Separate private and public sector sessions were first held to identify key issues and propose solutions from each perspective. These were followed by **joint public-private sessions** in each city to validate findings and co-design reforms. The convergence of views during these joint sessions marked a key success of the PPD, confirming a shared understanding of sectoral challenges and paving the way for joint ownership of policy outcomes.

The sessions drew participation from over **50 stakeholders** representing more than **25 institutions**, including the **Ministry of Transportation, General Authority for Roads and Bridges, Maritime Transport Authority, Libyan Civil Aviation Authority, municipal authorities, freight and logistics companies, shipping firms, port operators**, and regional chambers of commerce. The diverse representation ensured a holistic view of the sector's dynamics across road, maritime, and air transport.

Dialogue themes were centred around three priority areas:

- **Improving the Business Climate and Regulatory Framework**: Participants discussed outdated transport laws, inefficient customs and logistics procedures, and the fragmented institutional setup governing the sector. Proposals included streamlining regulations, establishing a unified national transportation strategy, and aligning infrastructure projects with broader economic development plans.
- **Integration into Regional and International Value Chains**: Libya's geographic potential as a transit hub for North Africa and the Mediterranean remains underutilized. Participants called for improved port efficiency, reform of procurement processes for infrastructure projects, and expansion of free trade zones beyond Misrata to enhance competitiveness.
- **Development of Urban and Non-Urban Transport**: The underdeveloped public transportation system, especially in urban areas, was highlighted as a major constraint. Stakeholders recommended investing in sustainable public transport, improving road safety, and introducing multimodal infrastructure planning aligned with climate and social inclusion goals—particularly to serve women and youth.

Concrete initiatives developed through the PPD included the establishment of a **national intermodal transport strategy**, the creation of **PPP-supported free zone logistics hubs**, and a roadmap for upgrading urban transit systems using green and inclusive design principles. These proposals were presented and validated at the **national PPD workshop in Tunis (29–30 November 2023)**, with a view toward implementation in partnership with both national stakeholders and international donors.

Through this process, the transportation PPD highlighted not only the urgency of reform but also the sector's untapped potential to act as a driver of sustainable and inclusive growth in Libya's fragile economic landscape.

Key Challenges Facing the Transportation Sector in Libya

The transportation sector in Libya is pivotal for economic recovery and growth but faces substantial challenges. These can be grouped into infrastructural deficits, security and regulatory issues, and workforce and environmental concerns.

Infrastructural and Economic Deficits

- **Degraded Infrastructure**: Prolonged conflicts have left Libya's transportation infrastructure in disrepair. A significant portion of roads and bridges have sustained damage, with the World Bank noting that the rehabilitation needs are acute, especially in conflict-affected areas where as much as 80% of transportation infrastructure requires urgent reconstruction (World Bank, 2023[7]).
- **Economic Dependency on Imports**: The IMF highlights Libya's reliance on imported goods, which places a strain on the existing transportation networks. In 2023, imports were reported to be approximately 20 times the volume of exports, demonstrating a heavy dependency that the current infrastructure cannot efficiently support (IMF, 2023[8]).

Security Challenges and Regulatory Weaknesses

- **Security Instability**: The transportation sector is severely impacted by ongoing security challenges, including the prevalence of checkpoints controlled by militias. These not only increase the risk of transit but also inflate costs due to widespread extortion. For instance, transport costs are reported to increase by up to 30% due to bribes and payments at illegal checkpoints (UN, 2023[30]).
- **Regulatory Fragmentation**: The lack of a unified regulatory framework complicates governance and hampers effective management of the transportation sector. The absence of consistent policy enforcement leads to operational inefficiencies and deters potential investment, critical for modernisation efforts.

Workforce and Technological Shortcomings

- **Shortage of Skilled Labor**: The sector suffers from a chronic shortage of skilled professionals due to the educational disruptions and emigration of trained personnel. This shortage is exacerbated by the country's instability, which discourages the return of skilled expatriates and impedes the training of new workforce entrants.
- **Technological Underutilisation**: There is a notable gap in adopting modern technologies that could enhance efficiency and integration within the sector. For example, digital logistics and fleet management systems are underutilised, hindering optimal routing, tracking, and delivery of goods.

Environmental Concerns and Public Transportation Needs

- **Environmental Impact**: Libya's transportation sector is a significant contributor to the nation's carbon footprint, with little to no adoption of green technologies. Initiatives for sustainable transportation, such as electric public buses or hybrid vehicles, are virtually non-existent.
- **Inadequate Public Transportation**: The public transportation system is underdeveloped and does not meet the mobility needs of the population, particularly in urban areas. This results in over-reliance on personal vehicles, contributing to urban congestion and increased environmental pollution. Enhancing public transit systems could alleviate these issues and provide a cleaner, more efficient alternative.

Figure 3.14. CO2 emissions by sector in selected MENA region countries

(ktCO2)

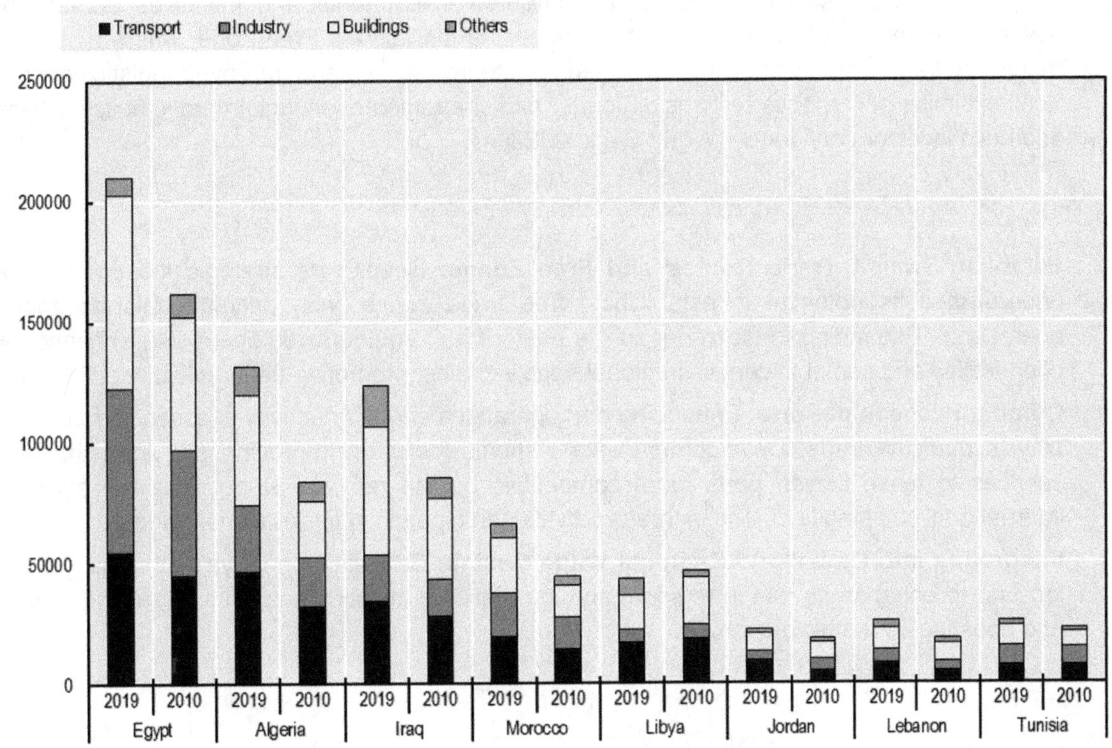

Strategic Priorities and Policy Recommendations for Libya's Transportation Sector

Policy Priority 1: Enhancing the Business Environment and Regulatory Framework

- **Strategic Transport Infrastructure Planning**: There is a critical need for a comprehensive transportation plan that integrates with urban development to support future economic growth. This plan should prioritise sustainable infrastructure development, leveraging Libya's geographic position to boost its role in trans-Mediterranean trade routes.
- **Facilitate Market Access for SMEs**: Improving logistics services such as trucking, warehousing, freight forwarding, and port management is crucial. According to the World Bank's Logistics Performance Index, Libya lags behind other MENA countries due to the quality of trade and transport-related infrastructure and the efficiency of clearance processes. Enhancing these areas will support Libya's trade and supply chain linkages with international markets, particularly benefiting smaller firms that currently face high transportation and insurance costs (World Bank, 2018). **Supporting Maritime and Airport Infrastructure**: Expand and modernise ports and airports to boost capacity and efficiency, enhancing Libya's role as a trade hub. Libya should prioritise the rehabilitation and modernisation of key ports (e.g. Tripoli, Misrata, Benghazi) and airports (e.g. Mitiga, Benina, Misrata) to improve capacity, safety, and efficiency. This includes upgrading cargo handling equipment, digitising customs and logistics systems, enhancing terminal infrastructure, and ensuring compliance with international standards. Strengthening these gateways

would reduce reliance on insecure overland routes, facilitate trade, and position Libya as a regional logistics hub in the southern Mediterranean (World Bank, 2023[7]).

- **Enhancing Governance and Regulatory Frameworks**: Develop a unified national transportation strategy to ensure well-coordinated and targeted investments and initiatives across various government and private entities. A clear example is the Misrata Free Zone, where a streamlined regulatory framework successfully attracted private investment and improved logistics operations. Scaling similar governance reforms nationally can strengthen oversight, improve policy coherence, and build investor confidence (World Bank, 2023[7]).

Policy Priority 2: Develop a Multimodal Transport Network

- **Establish Transit Trade Routes and Free Zones**: Despite its strategic location, Libya has underutilised its potential in establishing free trade zones, with only the Misrata zone fully operational. Expanding these zones in the eastern and southern regions would enhance Libya's connectivity and competitiveness in global supply chains, promoting economic diversification.
- **Competitiveness of Ports**: Enhancing port operations and connectivity is essential for increasing Libya's maritime trade. Development efforts should focus on improving port infrastructure and services to make Libyan ports more competitive on the regional stage. This will attract more international shipping lines and increase Libya's participation in international trade.
- **Integrating into Global and Regional Value Chains**: Capitalise on Libya's strategic geographic location to enhance its role in regional and international logistics networks, attracting investment and boosting economic growth.

Policy Priority 3: Develop Urban and Non-Urban Transportation Systems

- **Public Transportation Development**: Establishing a reliable, safe, and sustainable public transportation system is vital. Such development would address Libya's high per capita CO_2 emissions from the transport sector, which surpass those of neighbouring countries. A robust public transport system would also reduce traffic congestion, lower environmental impact, and support social and economic inclusion by improving access to education and employment, particularly for women and the youth.
- **Innovation in Transport**: Updating transport policies to accommodate technological innovations such as Mobility as a Service (MaaS) can transform public transport. By integrating various transport, information, and payment services, MaaS offers a seamless and efficient travel experience, which can significantly enhance the attractiveness and utility of public transport in Libya.
- **Improving Urban and Non-Urban Transport Networks**: Introduce eco-friendly public transportation options to mitigate environmental impacts and improve the quality of urban life, while simplifying logistics processes and enhancing trade facilitation to promote a more transparent and efficient transportation sector.

Conclusion and Implementation considerations

Revitalising Libya's transportation sector is crucial for economic recovery and long-term growth.

Short term: Immediate priorities include regulatory reforms to attract investment and infrastructure assessments, particularly for ports and airports. Launching pilot urban transportation projects will set benchmarks and build momentum for broader reforms.

Medium term: The focus should shift to large-scale infrastructure projects, including road and railway upgrades and integrating digital technologies for efficient transport management. Developing and operationalising free trade zones in strategic locations will strengthen Libya's role in global supply chains and support economic diversification.

Long term: Reforms should embed sustainable practices across all transport modes, aligning with global environmental standards. Policies must be continuously updated to integrate technological advancements and adapt to economic shifts, ensuring the sector remains a pillar of national development.

These reforms will modernise Libya's transport infrastructure, lowering costs, attracting investment, and boosting trade. A more efficient public transport system will also reduce carbon emissions, improve urban mobility, and enhance quality of life. However, Libya should be mindful of the need for clear governance, institutional coordination, and gradual implementation. Public-private dialogue can play a key role in identifying practical challenges and building consensus—for example, engaging logistics firms in shaping port reforms can help ensure solutions are both realistic and effective.

4 Summing up

Throughout the PPD process and from the various initiatives that have been identified within each sector, there are a number of themes that can be highlighted.

1. **Enhancing governance and supporting accountability**. To support an effective economic transition in Libya, there is a vital need to address the issue of state-owned enterprises and their dominance of certain sectors. This restructuring will not only ensure a more efficient delivery of services in the country but will also allow for the private sector to access these sectors and services. Furthermore, ensuring effective anti-corruption measures are put in place and implemented will support the restoring of trust between the two sectors.
2. **Reviewing legislation and regulatory policies**. There are a number of reforms that are being held back by outdated legislation which requires reform and modernisation. Involving the private sector in this reform process will ensure the adoption of legislation that takes into consideration the barriers that face the private sector.
3. **Ensuring transparent and sustained communication**. This is vital not only between the public and the private sectors, but also within the two sectors themselves. The challenges faced by the fragmentation of public institutions and the separate business associations has highlighted the need to rebuild formal communication structures that can help portray a unified voice and ensure closer coordination.
4. **Increased incentives for the private sector**. The conflict within the country and the impacts of COVID-19 demonstrated a resilient nature persistent within the private sector. This trait needs to be further nourished and supported so that the private sector can compete in regional and international markets, but also help contribute more effectively to the reconstruction efforts of the country.
5. **Promoting localised activities**. The geographical nature of the country demonstrates the need to have more localised and subnational approaches to private sector development to ensure all the various voices within the country are incorporated.

References

(n.a.) (n.d.), , http://documents.worldbank.org/curated/en/121101597261547774/Libya-Economic-Monitor-July-2020. [32]

Abughaighis, H., M. Tantoush and R. Hmedan (2018), *Challeneges and Needs of Youth in the Libyan Job Market*, Jusoor, http://jusoor.ly/wp-content/uploads/2018/10/SPARK-report-ENG-v4.pdf. [17]

CBL (2021), *4th Quarter Economic Bulletin*, Central Bank of Libya. [10]

FAO (2021), *Statistical Yearbook: World Food and Agriculture*, FAO, https://openknowledge.fao.org/server/api/core/bitstreams/522c9fe3-0fe2-47ea-8aac-f85bb6507776/content. [22]

FAO (2019), *Libya: The Impact of the Crisis on Agriculture*, Food and Agriculture Organization of the United Nations, https://api.godocs.wfp.org/api/documents/WFP-0000127069/download/?_ga=2.89230233.306782595.1745508354-864720658.1742567192. [20]

FAO and UNDP (2021), *Libya Agricultural Sector Overview*, FAO Report. [19]

Fitzgerald, M. (2018), "Socio-Political Situation in Libya from the Urban Perspective", *Notes internacionals CIDOB*, pp. 1-6, https://www.cidob.org/publicaciones/socio-political-situation-libya-urban-perspective. [5]

IMF (2023), *Libya - Selected Issues*, IMF, https://www.elibrary.imf.org/downloadpdf/journals/002/2023/202/article-A001-en.xml. [6]

IMF (2023), *Libya Selected Issues: Banking Sector Reform*, International Monetary Fund. [8]

Jordan Ministry of Digital Economy and Entrepreneurship (2021), "The National Digital Transformation Strategy & Implementation Plan (2021-2025)", https://www.modee.gov.jo/ebv4.0/root_storage/en/eb_list_page/dts-2021-eng.pdf. [31]

Juillard, H. et al. (2021), *Labour Market Assessment Libya*, IOM. [27]

OECD (2022), *Navigating beyond COVID-19: Recovery in the MENA Region*, OECD Publishing, Paris, https://doi.org/10.1787/48300c64-en. [28]

OECD (2021), "Enhancing connectivity through infrastructure investment", in *Middle East and North Africa Investment Policy Perspectives*, OECD Publishing, Paris, https://doi.org/10.1787/49d6211b-en. [25]

OECD (2021), *Ownership and Governance of State-Owned Enterprises: A Compendium of National Practices*, https://www.oecd.org/content/dam/oecd/en/publications/reports/2021/12/ownership-and-governance-of-state-owned-enterprises-2021_04e4bcaa/581de09d-en.pdf. [23]

OECD (2020), "Investment in the MENA region in the time of COVID-19", *OECD Policy Responses to Coronavirus (COVID-19)*, OECD Publishing, Paris, https://doi.org/10.1787/da23e4c9-en. [29]

OECD (2020), *The OECD Digital Government Policy Framework: Six dimensions of a Digital Government*, OECD Publishing, https://www.oecd.org/content/dam/oecd/en/publications/reports/2020/10/the-oecd-digital-government-policy-framework_11dd6aa8/f64fed2a-en.pdf. [14]

OECD (2017), *Benchmarking Digital Government Strategies in MENA Countries*, OECD Digital Government Studies, OECD Publishing, Paris, https://doi.org/10.1787/9789264268012-en. [33]

OECD (2017), *Getting Infrastructure Right, a Framework for Better Governance*, OECD Publishing, https://www.oecd.org/content/dam/oecd/en/publications/reports/2017/03/getting-infrastructure-right_g1g77a22/9789264272453-en.pdf. [24]

OECD (2016), *SMEs in Libya's Reconstruction: Preparing for a Post-Conflict Economy*, OECD Publishing, https://doi.org/10.1787/9789264264205-en. [15]

OECD (2016), *SMEs in Libya's Reconstruction: Preparing for a Post-Conflict Economy*, OECD Publishing, https://doi.org/10.1787/9789264264205-en. [3]

OECD (2007), *OECD Principles for Private Sector Participation in Infrastructure*, OECD Publishing, https://doi.org/10.1787/9789264034105-en. [26]

OECD/FAO (2018), *OECD-FAO Agricultural Outlook 2018-2027*, OECD Publishing, Paris/Food and Agriculture Organization of the United Nations, Rome, https://doi.org/10.1787/agr_outlook-2018-en. [34]

Pinaud, N. (ed.) (2007), *Public-Private Dialogue in Developing Countries, Opportunities and Risks*, OECD Development Sentre Studies, https://www.oecd.org/content/dam/oecd/en/publications/reports/2007/09/public-private-dialogue-in-developing-countries_g1gh8572/9789264028845-en.pdf. [4]

Rahman, A. and M. Di Maio (2020), *The Private Sector amid Conflict : The Case of Libya*, World Bank Group, http://documents.worldbank.org/curated/en/112031606288925984. [9]

REACH (2022), *Libya 2021 Multi-Sector Needs Assessment*, REACH Initiative, https://www.ecoi.net/en/file/local/2073499/REACH_LBY_report_LBY2105a_May2022.pdf. [12]

UN (2023), *UN Libya Results Report 2023*, https://libya.un.org/sites/default/files/2024-08/UN%20Libya%20Results%20Report%202023%20EN_0_0.pdf. [30]

UN (2021), *Libya, Common Country Analysis*. [2]

UN (2021), *Libya, Common Country Analysis*, United Nations, https://unsmil.unmissions.org/sites/default/files/un_libya_cca_2021_final_1.pdf. [36]

UNDP (2021), *Libya Labor Market Assessment*, https://www.undp.org/libya/publications/labour-market-assessment. [16]

Union, I. (ed.) (2021), *Global Cybersecurity Index*, https://www.itu.int/pub/D-STR-GCI.01. [18]

WFP (2020), *Libya Agricultrue and Livelihood Needs Assessment Report*, World Food Programme, https://api.godocs.wfp.org/api/documents/WFP-0000127069/download/?_ga=2.89230233.306782595.1745508354-864720658.1742567192. [21]

World Bank, W. (2023), *Libya Economic Monitor*, World Bank. [7]

World Bank, W. (2021), *Libya Economic Update October 2021*, World Bank, https://thedocs.worldbank.org/en/doc/a51575259a191dba4a5f9ac1e03f9eb9-0280012021/original/Libya-Economic-Update-October-2021.pdf?_gl=1*1l4fa4i*_gcl_au*MTk3MTc3NDgzMC4xNzI0NzYzMjkz. [1]

World Bank, W. (2019), *Libya Economic Monitor*, World Bank Group. [13]

World Bank, W. (2017), *Libya Economic Outlook*, World Bank Group. [11]

World Bank, W. (2009), *Doing Business 2010, Reforming through difficult times*, World Bank, https://www.doingbusiness.org/content/dam/doingBusiness/media/Annual-Reports/English/DB10-FullReport.pdf. [35]

Notes

[1] According to the OECD's States of Fragility report, Libya is categorised as a fragile state with severe vulnerabilities to resource dependency and unemployment rates. See: OECD (2022), States of Fragility 2022, OECD Publishing, Paris, https://doi.org/10.1787/c7fedf5e-en.

[2] Given the complexity of this sector and the perceived risks resulting from data security, and for the successful implementation of ICT reforms, technical support from research institutions, digital rights protection by civil society, and collaboration with international organisations such as the ITU and UNDP can be instrumental. The inclusion of these stakeholders can significantly enhance the design, credibility, and effectiveness of policy reform efforts.

www.ingramcontent.com/pod-product-compliance
Lightning Source LLC
LaVergne TN
LVHW060455061126
851857LV00016B/1838
9789264729605